MIDLAN
• TIMES •

CONTENTS

ISBN: 978-1-913251-53-6
First published in 2023 by Transport Treasury Publishing Ltd., 16 Highworth Close, High Wycombe HP13 7PJ

Copies of many of the images in MIDLAND TIMES are available for purchase/download.
In addition the Transport Treasury Archive contains tens of thousands of other UK, Irish and some European railway photographs.

www.ttpublishing.co.uk or for editorial issues and contributions email **MidlandTimes1884@gmail.com**

Printed in Malta by Gutenberg Press.

INTRODUCTION

Welcome to the second issue of Midland Times and thanks to those of you who wrote in with positive comments about issue 1. It is certainly a nervous time when a new publication is launched as you hope to have delivered a product that readers will enjoy.

Constructive criticism and observation is also welcomed and there's proof of that in the shape of correspondence from reader David Pearson of Haworth, West Yorkshire. It's in regard to the constituent list starting on page 4 of issue 1, concerning the operation and ownership of the County Donegal Railways Joint Committee lines. David has gone into great detail to explain the workings of this complex railway subject and we thank him for sending it in as it makes very interesting reading.

We, of course, have more interesting contributions for you to read accompanied by plenty of fantastic photographs from the vast Transport Treasury library.

With the recent Coronation of King Charles III it seems appropriate that we have been provided with two articles about the Coronation class. Whether you are a fan of the monarchy or not it's a good excuse to feature images of these magnificent locomotives that are favourites to many of us.

As well as this we cover quite a vast area of the country with subjects including a journey on the Callander and Oban Railway in the beautiful West Highlands of Scotland and a tour around the resorts of north Wales and north west of England that thirteen LMS Patriot locomotives were named after. There are also a couple of photographic articles, one of the railways around Stafford and another focusing on Beyer-Garratt locos to accompany the photo on the front cover of this issue. Add to those articles about Lord Stamp, appointed Chairman of the LMS in 1926, the amalgamation of the LNWR and LYR in 1922 and a lengthy article about the reorganisation of Crewe Works.

As mentioned before, we welcome your comments and if you would like to send a contribution in addition to those we have lined up for issue 3, we would welcome them in either written or image form.

PETER SIKES, EDITOR, MIDLAND TIMES
email: midlandtimes1884@gmail.com

ABOVE LEFT: Coronation Pacific NO. 46226 DUCHESS OF NORFOLK departs from Euston in this undated image. The locomotive is wearing the express blue livery which would date the picture between June 1951 and May 1954 before a repaint to green took place. Built by the LMS in May 1938 at a cost of £11,302 it was allocated to Camden (1B) on delivery, and was withdrawn in September 1964. © THE TRANSPORT TREASURY

FRONT COVER (AND INSET RIGHT):
Beyer-Garratt 2-6-0+0-6-2 No. 47982 pictured at Kettering on 7th May 1955. © THE TRANSPORT TREASURY

ROYAL CONNECTIONS

BY IAN LAMB

In the lead up to what was a globally momentous occasion – the Coronation of HM King Charles III – Hornby has appropriately produced a model of the BR 'Coronation' Class 8P 'Pacific' No. 46220 Coronation in blue livery as it was in 1953.

LMS 6220 *Coronation* was the first of the class to be constructed, emerging in streamlined form from Crewe Works in June 1937. The locomotive would have its casing removed in November 1946 at the same time as the replacement smoke deflectors were fitted. Nearly all its life it would be based at Glasgow Polmadie engine shed, primarily to haul express trains like 'The Royal Scot'.

The locomotive would go on to be withdrawn in April 1963 and was scrapped shortly after. Over its lifetime this engine wore five different liveries, briefly swap identities with classmate No. 6229 *Duchess of Hamilton* and hold the then locomotive world speed record of 114 miles per hour with Driver T. J. Clarke and Engineer Robert Riddles (whose name may be familiar) on the footplate.

This class of thirty-eight engines were in two halves, a streamlined version and a non-streamlined one, which even the former category would eventually be altered to make them all the same. The first five conventionally built locomotives were considered as 'Duchesses', numbered and named accordingly as No. 6230 *Duchess of Buccleuch* to 6234 *Duchess of Abercorn*. They appeared in 1938 with a single chimney and without smoke deflectors, and regarded by many (including myself) as the finest 'Pacific' engines ever built.

My favourite has always been *Duchess of Buccleuch*. I just loved the sheer size and bulk of these locomotives that in general terms all of them were worth writing about. However, whilst I had 'watched' them regularly rushing through Slateford and Kingsknowe or 'dead' at Polmadie, No. 46230 was the only one

The driver oils the motion of No. 6220 CORONATION. PHOTO: A. W. V. MACE © THE TRANSPORT TREASURY

12TH JULY 1952: The author's favourite Duchess NO. 46230 DUCHESS OF BUCCLEUCH pictured at Carstairs with 'The Royal Scot'. PHOTO: © THE TRANSPORT TREASURY

that I actually recorded travelling behind, and what a day it was.

Being the son of a railwayman – especially after the formation of British Railways at the beginning of 1948 – meant passes and privilege tickets. Such opportunities made it possible to visit engine sheds that were too far away to cycle, or would otherwise be outside pocket money limits, even on occasional journeys. Additionally Edinburgh (like most cities) had an 'Ian Allan Locospotters Club' based at Dalry Road, near to Princes Street station's main servicing depot. Engines allocated there were predominantly of LMS origin. I don't recall ever seeing a 'Duchess' on shed, but if they were unable to be reversed on the station's turntable, then they could go around the Coltbridge Triangle in which 64C Dalry Road was centred.

I couldn't have been long out of short trousers when I was allowed to join the locospotters club which meant a No. 3 tram ride into the city. Even though my personal interest at the time was strongly LNER – rather than LMS – now with British Railways being in vogue, the club programme covered all aspects of railways, and shed visits all over the place were organised, with occasional full day ventures involving long train journeys, such as to Newcastle and back.

One of these ventures was to Carlisle to visit four sheds: Upperby (LNWR); Durran Hill (Midland); Kingmoor (Caledonian) and Canal (NBR). Although once a year I was palmed off to relatives in Coventry for summer holidays, my 'West Coast' experience was very limited. Consequently, I was really looking forward to exploring the former 'Caledonian' main line, especially with a group of like-minded enthusiasts. The Sunday connecting service for Carlisle was with 'The Royal Scot' Glasgow-London express at the very 'way-out' village of Symington in the heart of the Upper Clyde Valley.

On meeting up at Princes Street station we were soon allocated to our reserved compartments, with the usual 'pecking

29TH FEBRUARY 1964: Near Kingsknowe station the Caledonian main line from Glasgow crossed the Union Canal. Around ten years later than my epic visit to Carlisle, Fairburn 2-6-4T No. 42273, of 64C Dalry Road, heads a similar local train to the one I was on to Symington. PHOTO: W. A. C. SMITH © THE TRANSPORT TREASURY

23RD JUNE 1953: The Royal Train believed to be approaching Kingsknowe station with NO. 46220 CORONATION in charge. PHOTO: © THE TRANSPORT TREASURY

LEFT: Symington Station island platform, attractively adorned for the Coronation. The track to the left was the alighting point for local trains, and also the one time junction for the cross-country route to Peebles.

order' of the biggest by the window. That didn't bother me too much, as I was simply engrossed in the Stanier coaches where the sliding compartment doors opened in two sections, the only design of coach that I had ever come across with this format.

Before boarding the relatively short train, time had been taken to espy the outline of a Fairburn 2-6-4T at the head, probably one of 64C Dalry Road's regulars. Often a 64D Carstairs tank engine would do the job, but as we would be travelling through the triangular junction there, so avoiding the station, and on to the main line for the short distance to Symington, it was more likely to have an Edinburgh source for motive power.

We were so excited on our 'day out' that we didn't pay much attention to the dull and dreary weather in Edinburgh, showing off its best 'Auld Reekie' mood. However, as the journey progressed, the rain became heavier. The misty windows in the coach corridor didn't allow much vision for the hope of any 'cops' in passing Dalry Road MPD. Our childish attempts at working out speed by noting the time between mileposts recorded a steady 35mph being maintained between Merchiston and Midcalder. Carstairs and Thankerton were soon past and I believe we arrived at Symington on time to await 'The Royal Scot'.

Standing on Symington platform was my biblical 'Road to Damascus' moment, the result of which shattered my parochial LNER heritage. The weather did not seem to be abating, with the wind blowing low and hard across the open moor. Tinto Hill (2,335 feet) was barely visible in the inclement gloom. The whole environment was sadly uninviting, and yet.

In the distance looking towards Carstairs one could gradually hear the pounding of a steam engine working hard up the hill from Glasgow. The sound increased as the train neared Symington, then all of a sudden there was silence before experiencing the most magnificent railway sight that I have ever seen when, emerging from out of the murk and mist, 'The Royal Scot' train gleamed like new as the heavy rain reflected brilliantly on a lean, green, steam machine matching a set of relatively new BR crimson and cream Mk1 coaches. The power and warmth of the locomotive as it slowly glided past me was overpowering. It was all hypnotic, and the scene has not dimmed in the memory over the years.

I was too numb to notice whether or not there was any slip when the driver opened the regulator to lift his heavy train on the long incline leading to Beattock Summit. By the time we reached Lockerbie the clouds started to break up and soon the late morning became brighter. The railway between Beattock and Ecclefechan takes advantage of Annandale – an almost flat belt of fields and trees tapering from a mile wide at Beattock to four miles wide at Ecclefechan – for gently curving track and high speed purposes. Glasgow and south western tracks merged with us at Gretna Junction before rushing into England over the River Stark with the bridge displaying two English and Scottish emblems respectively.

A girder bridge over the River Esk was crossed as the train slowed down at Etterbridge Junction on approach to Kingmoor, so the rush to obtain engine numbers in passing the depot was rather premature as they were obtained later in the day when visiting there. Carlisle Station has always impressed me; that day was no exception. Recalling memory is a strange experience. Ironically, I remember the visits to the sheds at Upperby and Durran Hill, but can make no recollection at all of the trips to Canal and Kingmoor, but I know I was there!

Between 1945 and 1950 the 'Royal Scot' was publicly non-stop between Glasgow Central and London Euston all year round. The 'Down' train halted at Kingmoor, whilst the 'Up' stopped beneath Carlisle No. 12 signalbox for crew change and engine examination. However, during winter 1950, the Carlisle Citadel station stop was reinstated.

Originally the whole class were ordered as streamlined, however the demands of maintaining the engines in that form far exceeded the cost savings in coal so the casings were eventually removed. In 1946 the next three 'Duchesses' (6253-6255) differed in appearance again, without the curved 'fall-plate' at the front, replaced with a split platform and smoke deflectors. The final 'as new' members of the class were 6256 and 6257, modified designs by Ivatt, featuring a different cab, pony truck, reversing gear and roller bearings.

De-streamlining of the remaining locomotives in the class began with No. 6235 *City of Birmingham* in April 1946, and

CORONATION DAY – 6TH JUNE 1953: Stanier 'Pacific' NO. 46220 CORONATION takes the curve at speed through Carstairs with 'The Royal Scot'. © TRANSPORT TREASURY

6243 *City of Lancaster* was the last in May 1949. Because the smokeboxes were angled down between the chimney and door to accommodate the sweep of the streamlined casing, this resulted in the engines concerned retaining that look. Eventually, the raked smokeboxes were replaced with conventional ones. By late 1958, the majority of the class showed a similar appearance, though all the defrocked engines retained the split platform 'utility' front end.

Polmadie MPD had many 'Princess Coronation' locomotives, and missing from the trio that I was mainly familiar with was *Duchess of Atholl*. I was too young to appreciate LMS red, and feel strongly that the class was vastly improved once 'shields' (smoke deflectors) were fitted. Nevertheless – though green with envy – my best friend in Galashiels in the Borders had the Hornby-Dublo three-rail locomotive plus two tin-plate coaches (all in LMS maroon) and let me play with them!

Along with the LNER 'Coronation' train between Edinburgh and London, both services deserve to be remembered as the zenith of long-distance steam-hauled express operating in Britain.

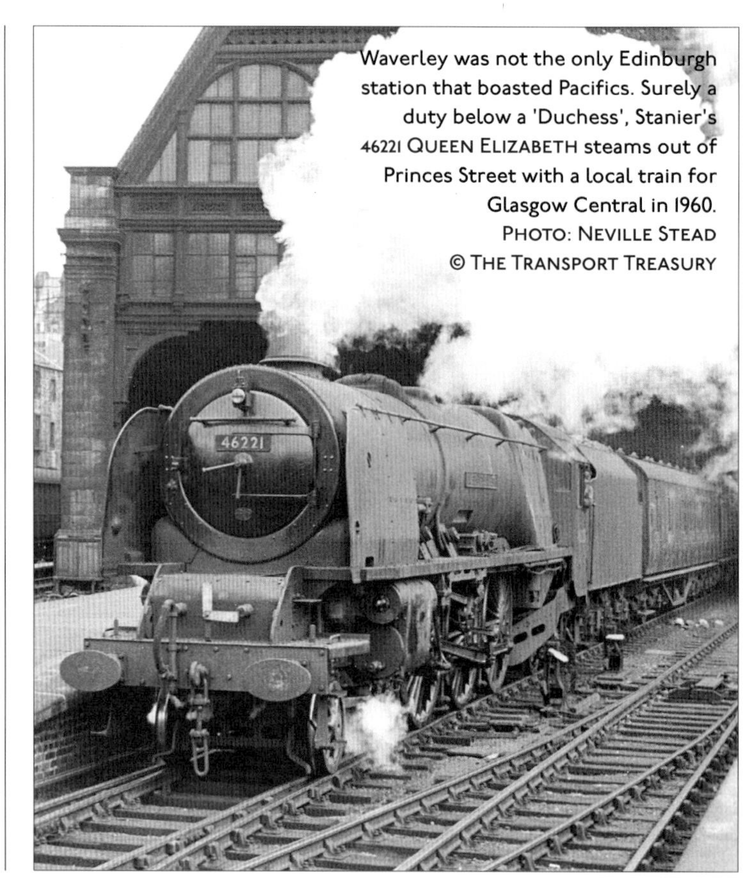

Waverley was not the only Edinburgh station that boasted Pacifics. Surely a duty below a 'Duchess', Stanier's 46221 QUEEN ELIZABETH steams out of Princes Street with a local train for Glasgow Central in 1960. PHOTO: NEVILLE STEAD © THE TRANSPORT TREASURY

10TH MARCH 1956: Princess Coronation Class 4-6-2 NO. 46220 CORONATION in immaculate condition heading the Up 'Royal Scot' passes Polmadie yard in Glasgow. PHOTO: W. A. C. SMITH © THE TRANSPORT TREASURY

AROUND STAFFORD IN THE LATE STEAM AGE

WORDS AND PHOTOS BY ALAN POSTLETHWAITE

Between college years, I did six months of industrial training with English Electric, Stafford. As a Southern man with limited knowledge of the LMS, I soon became entranced by the Wolverhampton line, also by Stafford itself and the Trent Valley lines. I arrived during the Great Freeze of 1963 which lasted from the beginning of January until mid-April. I can still feel the chilblains!

The first photos here show the frozen landscape from which I escaped, chilled to the bone, into the relative warmth of a Midland Red Bus (with rear doors). As the weather became warmer, I explored further afield to the North Staffordshire Railway and to the GWR-LNWR joint lines from Shrewsbury. Most intriguing was the Great Northern branch from Uttoxeter to Stafford which had no right to exist – but then neither did the LNWR line to Peterborough. Competition was rife during the Railway Mania, however risky the investment.

South of Stafford, a Stanier Mogul heads some remarkably clean coaches on a beeline to Wolverhampton.

The first (closed) station south of Stafford was Penkridge. I was privileged to be invited into the signal box by signalman Mr. A. Hunt. The LNWR lever frame is characterised by the loop-handles for the catch rods and a separate rear-board for the lever nameplates. Other features are the track diagram, telephone, two oil lamps, a tall desk with the train register, a tin of Nescafé on the stool and age-distorted window glass.

South of Stafford station, guarding the junction to London and Wolverhampton, were two majestic wooden LNWR signal brackets with pressed-steel LMS arms. On the left are goods reception sidings. On the right is a local goods yard. Centre-stage, Black Five No. 45441 heads a train of container wagons.

A DMU cruises towards Stafford station.

Stafford MPD could be observed from the platforms of the station. In the foreground we see Standard 5MT No. 73025 with Stanier 2-6-4 tank No. 42546 at the coaling stage.

The LNWR wooden Outer Home signal bracket off the Wolverhampton line was over 50 feet tall.

An unlikely set of coaches on a Stafford siding: on the right, two BR sleeping cars; on the left, part of an EMU built by Siemens in 1914 for the LNWR shuttle between Willesden Junction and Earls Court. In 1951, such stock was transferred to the Midland Railway's Lancaster to Heysham branch for BR electrification trials at 50 Hz.

Black Five 4-6-0 No. 45114 pictured on the Wolverhampton line with a short train which includes a Palethorpe's sausage van.

Part of a Midland Railway coach in Stafford goods yard.

LMS 'Crab' No. 42939 passes through the landscape on the quadruple main line between Stafford and Colwich Junction with a mixed freight.

A Down fitted parcels train speeds through the (closed) Colwich station. The building is in the Jacobean style of the North Staffordshire Railway whose Trent Valley line commences here on the right.

Beneath new catenary arms near Colwich Junction, Britannia class Pacific NO. 70031 BYRON, heads an express to Euston.

LORD STAMP AND THE LMS

BY JEREMY CLEMENTS

Railway management in the first 60-odd years of the 20th Century was typified by respect for tradition and by a strong strain of conservatism at all levels. Among senior career railwaymen, instances of innovative and successful action to tackle changing market conditions were comparatively few. Sam Fay's rescue of the Great Central from impending financial difficulties and Herbert Walker's electrification programme for the London & South Western/ Southern systems were comparatively rare examples of creative forward thinking on a grand scale. On the other hand, radical industry reformation – for better or for worse – depended in certain cases upon outsiders who brought to bear skills and experiences gathered elsewhere in confronting pressing issues, and in implementing solutions that traditionalists would never have dared contemplate. Two individuals in this category were Sir Guy Granet and Lord Stamp (Dr. Richard Beeching was a third example who fortunately lies outside the scope of this article).

Granet (1867-1943) was educated at Balliol College, Oxford and called to the bar in 1893. Seven years later he was appointed Secretary of the Railway Companies' Association and from there moved in 1905 to become General Manager of the Midland Railway, a most unusual career path at that time. Over the following eight years, his abilities and analytical skills were deployed in successful reorganisation of the MR's freight business under the supervision of Cecil Paget as General Superintendent. Granet's attitude towards motive power development was less progressive by resisting investment in larger locomotives, thereby contributing to CME R. E. Deeley's early departure.

Prior to World War 1, Granet had starred as an expert witness in parliamentary committees and his services were called upon by the government during the conflict. He was appointed Controller of Import Restrictions, then Deputy Director of Military Railways at the War Office, and finally Director-General of Movements and Railways. His talents and his experience as a Whitehall 'insider' were complemented by a Machiavellian ability to get his own way. Post-war, he is believed to have played a major role behind the scenes in the debate between nationalisation and reorganisation under continued private ownership, and was then influential in the shaping of the Big Four. He gave up his position as chief executive officer of the Midland Railway in 1918 and took a seat on that company's board. At the Grouping, he became deputy Chairman of the London, Midland & Scottish Railway, and then Chairman from 1924 to 1927.

Despite his apparent success in fashioning the new LMS, allegedly to favour ex-MR interests, Granet apparently could do little to remove the major and petty issues that derived from pre-Grouping rivalries. As with the MR twenty years earlier, an outsider was needed to orchestrate the change process so Granet arranged the appointment of Sir Josiah Stamp as Chairman (later President) of the LMS from 1926.

JOSIAH CHARLES STAMP (1880-1941)

A native of Hampstead, London and educated in Goudhurst, Kent, he joined the Inland Revenue Service as a boy clerk aged sixteen years and rose to become an Assistant Secretary in that service by 1916. Concurrently, he pursued tertiary education as an external student achieving a first class honours degree at the University of London in 1911 and a doctorate at the London School of Economics in 1916. His PhD thesis, published as British Incomes and Property became a standard work and cemented his academic reputation.

In 1919 he left the Inland Revenue to become a Director and Secretary of Nobel Industries, a forerunner of Imperial Chemical Industries Ltd., and in 1928 he was appointed a director of the Bank of England. During the inter-war years he served on numerous public commissions, committees and boards, and was widely respected for the scope of his knowledge and for his erudition. He was considered a polymath whose career embraced industrialist, economist, civil servant, taxation expert, statistician, writer, central banker and company director. He was also Colonel commanding the Royal Engineers Railway and Transport Corps (1927-41) and Honorary Colonel of Transportation Units in the Royal Engineers Supplementary Reserve (1938-1941). He was appointed a Knight of the Order of the British Empire in 1920 and a Knight Grand Cross of the Bath in 1936.

There was dreadful irony in his passing as among his various governmental appointments, he had served on the Dawes

Reparation Commission on German Currency and Finance which led to his becoming in 1935 a founder member of the Anglo-German Fellowship. He made low key visits to Germany in 1936 (when he met Hitler) and in 1937 to view the Nazi Party Congress, with the tacit approval of the Foreign Secretary. With the outbreak of war, he was viewed by some as an 'appeaser' which sobriquet was then highly unpopular. Having been raised to the peerage in 1938 as Baron Stamp, he was killed together with his wife and elder son on 16th April 1941 when his home at Shortlands, Kent suffered a direct hit during the Blitz.

THE LMS AS A BUSINESS

The Grouping created the London Midland & Scottish Railway as the largest of the Big Four. Its dominant position was evident in its percentage shares of the UK railway sector:

As at 31 December 1923	% total
Route miles	36
Track miles including sidings	39
Steam locomotives	43
Passenger coaches	41
Seating capacity	41
Wagon fleet numbers	43
Total passenger receipts	38
Total freight receipts	44
Total freight tonnage	39
Total employees	41
Median	40

By any standard, the LMS was an enormous enterprise, unmatched by any other commercial undertaking in the country. Post-war industry reorganisation had been inevitable but the complex legal task of joining together different companies under a single ownership was dwarfed by the challenge of making the new giant operate harmoniously and efficiently. An organisation mired in pre-1923 tribal cultures risked failure to cope with prevailing demands and thus a rare level of outside talent was required to enact reform.

In addressing a daunting task, Stamp needed his experience as a business manager and as a statistician to assess the company's position in the broader market context, i.e. inland transport as a whole. Growing wealth during the 1920s (excluding the troubled General Strike year of 1926) was reflected in burgeoning enthusiasm for road transport. This was followed by the Depression of 1931-33 which adversely affected all modes of transport and general economic activity, and then by steady recovery from 1934 onwards. The trading revenue of the Big Four during this period:

£m	LMS		LNER		SR		GWR	
Year	Passenger	Freight	Passenger	Freight	Passenger	Freight	Passenger	Freight
1923	26	47	17.5	36	14.8	6.1	10.6	18.3
1930	20.4	40.4	13.5	33.5	14.1	5.6	9	17
1933	17.8	33.3	11.5	26.5	12.6	4.8	7.5	13.9
1937	20.4	39.6	13.1	31.1	14.7	4.9	8.5	16.4

Apart from fluctuations driven by economic circumstance, more insidious influences with long-lasting impact were at work in the road transport sector:

Year	Motorcycles	Cars, omnibuses	Goods vehicles
1923	430,000	469,000	173,000
1930	724,000	1,157,000	348,000
1933	563,000	1,288,000	387,000
1937	488,000	1,884,000	478,000

Growing affluence had an impact on composition of the road market e.g. the motorcycle population peaked at 731,000 in 1929 before declining as travellers sought the luxury provided by four wheels. The combination of wealth, comfort and convenience had a particular effect upon the proportions by volume of railway passenger ticket sales:

Year	Full fare	Exc./ wkd.	Work-men	Season tickets	Other	Total revenue
1923	31.5%	9.6%	18%	34.6%	6.3%	£70.3m
1930	11.9%	33%	18.1%	32.7%	4.3%	£58.6m
1933	7.9%	39%	17.5%	31.7%	4.2%	£51.1m
1937	6.5%	40%	18.6%	30.7%	4%	£59.5m

The shrinkage in full tariff sales was profound. Even allowing for then prevalent deflation, the real value of passenger unit sales showed marked deterioration with 93.5% of the 1937 total achieved through some form of discount mechanism. The average retail value of individual ticket sales declined while aggregate volumes remained more or less static.

Freight traffic formed the industry's greatest revenue source. Unfortunately, gross income was closely tied to trading volumes by virtue of fixed pricing structures that bound the railways through their legal obligation as common carriers. Operations were also burdened by the incubus of the notorious private owner wagon system whose embedded inefficiencies contributed to lamentable returns on fixed and mobile assets. Industry-wide freight movements reflected another worrying element:

	1923	1930	1933	1937
Tonnage conveyed (millions)	420	374	310	365
Gross receipts (£ millions)	107.4	96.5	78.5	92
Receipts per ton-mile (pence)	1.5	1.4	1.4	1.3

The most ominous trend was in receipts per ton-mile where underlying earnings steadily declined. A major factor was the motor lorry population which grew 2¾ times between 1923 and 1937 as independent operators exploited the convenience of door-to-door delivery to cherry-pick the most profitable business opportunities.

The macro issues and challenges confronting Stamp were of a scale and complexity far removed from the parochial attitudes associated with the constituent companies. These might be summarised at operating level in alternative philosophies e.g. a heavy train hauled by a red 4-4-0 automatically necessitated a pilot locomotive whereas its black counterpart would solve the problem with a bout of hard thrashing.

SOLUTIONS

The British railway network was blessed (or cursed) with a lavishly capitalised fixed infrastructure that had grown like topsy either through competitive forces or through satisfaction of local civic expectations. Many structures contributed to superb route grading and alignment which over the years rendered a financial return in the form of smaller locomotives in relation to train loads than would otherwise have been necessary. The case was often weak for ornate and imposing stations built for passenger traffic that had never materialised or had been bled away by later competing railways or other means of transport. Poor asset utilisation is photographically evident from the Big Four era (and of course later) in portrayal of trains standing at grandiose stations where the human element (passengers) is sadly absent.

As a rough rule of thumb, a railway company's infrastructural investment accounted for about 50% of the book value of total capital assets. For Stamp, the static nature of this 'wealth' prevented its mobilisation or redeployment except in marginal instances and it was only in Beeching's time that drastic surgery in asset realisation would take place, with all its concomitant implications. Thus about half the assets were static, immovable and often financially under-performing. Measures to improve the company's fortunes could only be found through enhanced operational effectiveness that yielded better returns on the mobile fixed assets. This exercise was desirable both economically and in eradication of the pre-Grouping rivalries that had prevented development of the company's administrative structure in a collegiate sense.

There was precedent in a successful management partnership during pre-Grouping times for what followed. Sam Fay, as General Manager of the financially-challenged Great Central was an atypical career railwayman of that era – forceful, visionary, dynamic, imaginative. His effectiveness was enhanced by his close working collaboration with John G. Robinson who had preceded him by joining the company as Chief Mechanical Engineer some 18 months earlier in 1900. Their joint efforts strove to improve operating standards in the GCR's vast freight business and while considerable progress was achieved, that company was still not fully 'in the clear' when its independence was subsumed at the Grouping.

With Stamp, progress had much to do with recruitment of a new CME to overhaul mobile fixed assets. William Stanier was one of two truly outstanding CMEs of the Big Four era (the other was Richard Maunsell who achieved wonders with resources severely limited by Herbert Walker's commitment to electrification). Stanier embraced all aspects of the CME's responsibilities and his holistic approach encompassed far more than mere headline-grabbing with a cadre of pampered pacifics. He recognised the totality of his obligations in a commercial as well as engineering sense in response to strictures imposed by Stamp.

Fleet rationalisation which had started in the 1920s was sustained through Stanier's massive re-stocking programme and the percentage reduction achieved in the review period was remarkable:

Locomotive fleet totals:	1923	1930	1933	1937	% reduction 1923 > 1937
LMS	10,289	9,319	8,225	7,657	26
LNER	7,388	7,316	6,901	6,576	11
GWR	3,944	3,801	3,754	3,632	8
SR	2,258	2,023	1,927	1,814	20

Only the SR came close to matching the LMS performance but this was largely by steam fleet attrition through electrification. On the LMS between 1931 and 1937, the ratio of locomotive withdrawals to new construction was about 2.7 to 1. This progress was achieved through a broader approach than just scrap-and-build as Stanier pursued improvements on several fronts and two examples serve to illustrate this point.

Imported from the GWR was the low-superheat boiler policy which was applied to the early Jubilee 4-6-0s. Different types of boiler were tried as, to Swindon's undisguised glee, steaming and some reliability problems were encountered. Nonetheless, twenty engines with the original Jubilee boilers achieved mileages of 70,000-77,000 miles p.a. and career annual averages with the class varied between 41,000 and 64,000. Comparative career annual averages for GWR Castles varied between c. 32,000 (No. 7008) and c. 50,000 (No. 4080).

Reforms in motive power policy extended to older and second-tier types where some impressive increases in average annual motive power mileages resulted:

Class	1927-30	1936	% increase
Ex-LNWR Prince of Wales	31,830	38,210	20
4-6-0 Royal Scot	54,970	72,250	31
2-6-0 Crab	30,730	40,440	32

Stanier adopted a multi-faceted approach in improving returns on the company's motive power investment (and in the process proved that he was the finest CME that the GWR never had). His success was doubtless with the encouragement of Stamp's considerable commercial acumen. With this sort of performance, the latter must have been well satisfied in his choice of CME and he seems to have been content to leave mechanical engineering and related policies almost entirely in Stanier's hands. Stamp did however pass a well-remembered remark to the effect that he saw little point in spending time keeping locomotives clean, providing that they were up to the task in hand. This may have been an affront to observer enthusiasm but he was more concerned with commercial efficiency to keep a major enterprise in sound financial health.

Statistics in this article have been taken from the survey published 1st June 1938 by The Railway Research Service of 4 Cowley Street, Westminster, London SW1, and from publications by the Railway Correspondence & Travel Society.

BELOW: One of the class of locos with improved average mileage, as described in the table opposite, Hughes/Fowler 'Crab' Class 5MT No. 42886 is pictured at Crewe with Stanier 'Black Five' No. 44782 at the opposite platform.
PHOTO: A. W. V. MACE © TRANSPORT TREASURY

THE LNWR AND LYR AMALGAMATION OF 1922

BY GERALD BEALES AND MIKE MUSSON

In a letter addressed to the Proprietors of the London and North Western Railway, headed 'Future of Railways' and dated 19th May 1921, Deputy Chairman C. N. Lawrence described the outcome of negotiations between the Railway Companies' Association and the Minister of Transport, Sir Eric Geddes, concerning the Government's intended grouping of railways in the aftermath of the Great War. Lawrence's letter referred to 'constant and arduous negotiations... taking place' between the RCA and the Government, following publication of the latter's White Paper on the subject, resulting in 'considerable modification' of the Government's proposals, ultimately set out in a Bill submitted to Parliament on 11th May 1921.

Under the terms of the Bill, Lawrence explained: 'The Railways are to be formed into groups by a process of amalgamation and absorption... the grouping to come into operation on the first day of January 1923.'

Lawrence went on: 'The Bill provides for the undertaking of the London and North Western Company together with those of the Midland, Lancashire and Yorkshire, North Stafford, and Furness Companies and certain other small subsidiary Companies being formed into one group.'

Lawrence pointed out, however, that the Companies were 'free to propose any scheme of grouping according to their own choice, alternative to that of the Bill, the option extending up to the 30th June 1922, and that scheme shall be approved by the Minister unless, in his opinion, it is incompatible with the economical and efficient working of the railway systems. Both Houses of Parliament must also assent to the alteration.'

In fact, the LNWR had already decided on a step towards the Government's proposed grouping, and communicated that decision to its shareholders, before Lawrence's letter was written. In an earlier letter addressed 'To the Proprietors of the London and North Western Railway', dated 5th April 1921, Secretary J. Bishop wrote: 'I am instructed by the Directors to inform you that, subject to the approval of the Proprietors, they have entered into a provisional Agreement with the Directors of the Lancashire and Yorkshire Railway Company under which, from a date to be agreed, that undertaking will be acquired by the London and North Western Company.'

Bishop's letter set out in detail the financial terms of the agreement, by which holders of LYR stock were to receive LNWR stock in exchange; and it was proposed that a number of LYR Directors should join the LNWR Board. The L&Y Secretary, R. C. Irwin, addressed a similar letter, on the same date, 'To the Proprietors of the Lancashire & Yorkshire Railway'.

So why did the LNWR jump the gun in this way, subjecting itself to the trouble and cost of an arrangement with the LYR that would come into effect just one year before both Companies were to be absorbed into what became the LMS? As Bishop's letter went on to point out: 'For very many years past the interests of the two Companies have been closely allied. As far back as 1873 proposals were made for a formal amalgamation, but Parliament refused its sanction. Closer working was, however, to some extent obtained by means of various arrangements for pooling competitive traffic'. It certainly seems to have been the case that, in Lancashire and the West Riding of Yorkshire, where the lines of the LYR and the LNWR were closely intertwined, the prevailing spirit between the two Companies had become very much one of co-operation rather than competition. But the effect of creating a 'Greater LNWR' in this way was presumably also seen as a means of placing the LNWR in a stronger position vis-à-vis the Midland (which had enhanced its own position by the acquisition of the London, Tilbury and Southend Company before the Great War) as arrangements for the new LMS undertaking were negotiated.

The amalgamation also gave the LNWR access to the best LYR 'talent', to replace some of its own departing senior officers.

ARTHUR WATSON – GENERAL MANAGER

Arguably, the process of amalgamation of the LNWR and the LYR began on 1st January 1921, with the appointment of Arthur Watson as General Manager of the LNWR, following the retirement (and election to the Board) of Sir Thomas Williams.

The L&NWR Gazette of January 1921 welcomed Mr. Watson in enthusiastic terms.

'The appointment of Mr. Arthur Watson, C.B.E., M.Inst.C.E., M.Inst.T. as general manager of the L.&N.W. Railway, which position he will hold in addition to that of general manager of the L.&Y. Railway, constitutes an event of considerable importance in the railway world. For one individual to attain to the leading executive position in two of our large railways is in itself a notable achievement, but coming as it does at a time when the future of British railways is an all absorbing matter, it suggests a possibility of symptomatic value, which gives an added general interest to the appointment. From the point of view of the staffs of the two concerns there is the great advantage that while we, on the L.&N.W., welcome a new chief, our comrades on the L.&Y. Railway are not called upon to say farewell to their present head – we and they have become colleagues, a fact of which we, for our parts, are proud.

'Mr. Watson is a Manchester man, having been born in that city in 1873. He was educated at the Manchester Grammar School and the Victoria University, Manchester, and in 1890 he was articled as civil engineer to the Chief Engineer of the Lancashire and Yorkshire Railway... On the retirement, in January, 1919, of Sir John Aspinall, Mr. Watson was selected to succeed him as (LYR) general manager...

'On behalf of our readers, we beg to offer to our new general manager sincerest congratulations, to which we venture to add an assurance of loyalty and service, and an endeavour on the part of us all to make his association with the L.&N.W. Railway something he can look upon with the maximum of satisfaction.'

REORGANISATION

It must be assumed that Arthur Watson, with his considerable existing knowledge of the LYR, played a large part, over the following year, in planning the reorganisation of the two Companies, in terms both of structure and personnel.

The L&NWR Gazette of December 1921 recognised that this was a time of uncertainty for the staff involved.

'Subject to the approval of the Railways Amalgamation Tribunal, the L.&Y. Company will cease to have a separate existence, as from 1st January, 1922, and will be completely merged in the London & North Western Railway. This will be the first step in the process of grouping, which will form such an important part of railway life and activity during the next few months. To those concerned directly as servants of the two railways, the immediate future is of interest, real and personal, for in times of change many things may occur. These things, however, will have to remain until the time of revelation arrives – speculation, like rumours, being more unsettling than satisfying.'

In fact, the 'servants of the two railways' did not have long to wait for 'the time of revelation' – at least as far as the main restructuring of the amalgamated Companies was concerned.

In December 1921, General Manager Arthur Watson produced a pocket-sized booklet (right) entitled 'Reorganisation of Railway 1922', which set out the structure of the enlarged LNWR; and Watson also used the January 1922 issue of the L&NWR Gazette to supply details to ex-LYR and LNWR staff.

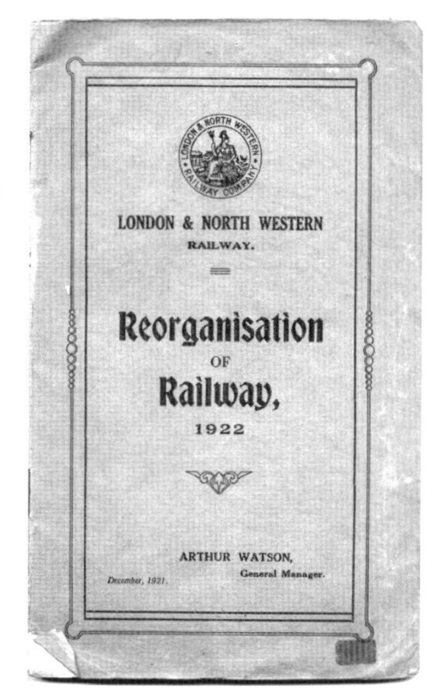
LONDON & NORTH WESTERN RAILWAY.

Reorganisation OF Railway, 1922

ARTHUR WATSON, General Manager.

December, 1921.

R. C. Irwin, (bottom right) who had been Secretary of the LYR since July 1899, was appointed Secretary of the enlarged LNWR; and the post-amalgamation Company was split into two divisions based on geographical areas. Crewe itself and all lines south of that point became the Southern Division of the enlarged LNWR; the Northern Division comprised everything north of Crewe, including ex-LYR lines.

THE DIVISIONAL GENERAL SUPERINTENDENTS' DEPARTMENT

The post of Divisional General Superintendent of the Southern Division went to Lancelot Horne MVO CBE, who first joined the LNWR in 1893. The Divisional General Superintendent of the Northern Division was Ashton Davies MBE, a Lancashire and Yorkshire Railway man, who was said to be well liked and highly respected by his colleagues and subordinates. Davies kept his

To the Proprietors of the London and North Western Railway.

LONDON & NORTH WESTERN RAILWAY,
SECRETARY'S OFFICE,
EUSTON STATION, LONDON, N.W.1.
5th *April*, 1921.

DEAR SIR (OR MADAM),

I am instructed by the Directors to inform you that, subject to the approval of the Proprietors, they have entered into a provisional Agreement with the Directors of the Lancashire & Yorkshire Railway Company under which, from a date to be agreed, that undertaking will be acquired by the London & North Western Company.

For very many years past the interests of the two Companies have been closely allied. As far back as 1873 proposals were made for a formal amalgamation, but Parliament refused its sanction. Closer working was, however, to some extent obtained by means of various arrangements for pooling competitive traffic, the latest Agreement having been entered into by the Lancashire & Yorkshire, London & North Western, and Midland Railway Companies in 1909, for a period of not less than 100 years.

Recent events have convinced the Directors of the two Companies concerned that public opinion on the question of amalgamation has changed, and this fact, together with the expressed approval by the Government of the principle of grouping, has resulted in negotiations which have led up to the present Agreement, which the Directors believe will be in the best interests of the Proprietors of the two Companies.

The terms of the Agreement, which will be subject to the approval of the Proprietors, and to obtaining through Parliament the necessary sanction, are that the Prior Stocks of the Lancashire & Yorkshire Company shall be exchanged into the following Prior Stocks of the London & North Western Company. The yield in Interest or Dividend will be the same amount as hitherto, with the exception of the L. & Y. 6% Minimum Preference and the 4½% Minimum Preference Stocks, the holders of which will receive in respect of each £100 of such Stocks an additional £6 5s. 0d. and £12 10s. 0d. respectively of L. & N. W. 4% Guaranteed Stock, for the surrender of existing contingent rights.

L. & Y. Stock.		L. & N. W. Stock to be issued in exchange.	
For each :—			
£100 3% Debenture Stock ...		£100 0 0	3% Debenture Stock.
£100 6% Minimum Preference Stock	£150 0 0 plus 6 5 0		4% Guaranteed Stock, Ditto for surrender of contingent rights.
		£156 5 0	
£100 4½% Minimum Preference Stock	£112 10 0 plus 12 10 0		4% Guaranteed Stock, Ditto for surrender of contingent rights.
		£125 0 0	
£100 4% Guaranteed Stock ...		£100 0 0	4% Guaranteed Stock.
£100 3% Preference Stock ...		£75 0 0	4% Preference Stock.
£100 4% Preference Stock (1903)		£100 0 0	4% Preference Stock (1902).
£100 4% Preference Stock (1908)		£100 0 0	4% Preference Stock (1902).
£100 5% Redeemable Preference Stock (1916), Redeemable 30/6/1926		£100 0 0	5% Redeemable Preference Stock, Redeemable same date.

The Holders of Lancashire & Yorkshire Ordinary Stock will receive in exchange for each **£100** of such Stock **£73** London & North Western Ordinary Stock.

It is proposed that a certain number of the Directors of the Lancashire & Yorkshire Company shall be elected upon the Board of the London & North Western Company.

A Meeting of the Proprietors will be summoned at a later date, when the proposed terms and conditions will be submitted for their approval.

Yours faithfully,
J. BISHOP,
Secretary.

Letters addressed to the Proprietors of the London and North Western Railway from Secretary, J. Bishop and Deputy Chairman, C. N. Lawrence, dated 5th April 1921 and 19th May 1921 respectively. (LNWRS CORR0202/CORR0201)

IMPORTANT.

London and North Western Railway.

EUSTON STATION,
LONDON, N.W. 1.
19th May, 1921.

DEAR SIR (OR MADAM),

FUTURE OF RAILWAYS.

On the 18th December, 1920, the Chairman forwarded to the Proprietors copy of a communication addressed to Sir Eric Geddes setting out the observations of the Railway Companies' Association on the proposals of the Minister of Transport as contained in the "White Paper"; and at the Annual General Meeting held on the 25th February last I explained the position of matters as they then stood, and informed the Proprietors of the intention of the Government to bring in a Bill at an early date.

Since that Meeting constant and arduous negotiations have been taking place between the Railway Companies' Association and the Government, with the result that considerable progress has been made towards the composing of differences which had arisen, and the Bill as introduced by the Minister on the 11th instant shows a considerable modification in many respects of the scheme as outlined in the White Paper.

The main principles of the Bill are as follows:—

(1) The Railways are to be formed into groups by a process of amalgamation and absorption, on terms to be agreed, or failing agreement, to be determined by a tribunal, the grouping to come into operation on the first day of January, 1923.

The Bill provides for the Undertaking of the London and North Western Company together with those of the Midland, Lancashire and Yorkshire, North Stafford, and Furness Companies, and certain other small subsidiary Companies being formed into one group.

The Companies are, however, free to propose any scheme of grouping according to their own choice, alternative to that of the Bill, the option extending up to the 30th June, 1922, and that scheme shall be approved by the Minister unless, in his opinion, it is incompatible with the economical and efficient working of the railway system. Both Houses of Parliament must also assent to the alteration.

2

(2) In regard to finance, the Government refused to entertain the suggestion that the guarantee of the 1913 net receipts should be extended for a period beyond the 15th August next, but they have agreed to place at the disposal of the Companies in Great Britain a sum of £60,000,000 in settlement of the claims arising out of the control, and that sum will be allocated amongst the Companies on a scheme of apportionment set forth in the Bill, and will be available for the general requirements of the Companies.

(3) The provisions as to the future regulation of the Railways, including the gradual standardisation of plant and equipment, which have been inserted in the Bill, represent very substantial modifications of the original proposals of the Minister.

(4) The provisions for the new rate fixing machinery are on the lines generally of the Report of the Rates Advisory Committee. Rates are to be fixed so as to secure to the Companies a standard revenue equivalent to the net receipts of 1913 plus allowances for recent capital expenditure, for unfructified capital, and also to cover whatever may have to be paid for interest on fresh capital. In addition, the formula for future adjustment of rates is so stated that if and as working expenses fall, and granted improved trade conditions, the amalgamated Companies will be enabled to attain by gradual steps a higher level of earning power.

(5) The clauses as to management provide that the Directors of the new amalgamated Companies shall be qualified Proprietors, elected by the Proprietors.

In regard to wages and conditions of service, effect is given to the arrangements which have been arrived at by negotiation between the Railway Companies and the Trade Unions whereby it has been agreed to continue (unless otherwise determined by 12 months' notice) the Central and National Wages Boards, and to establish for each group Councils composed of officers and elected employees whose functions will be generally on the lines of the Whitley Report on Industrial Councils.

This is an arrangement which your Board believes will operate both in the interests of the Shareholders and the Staff. It also provides suitable machinery for the adjustment of labour questions on economic lines, and should be of material help in the settlement of such questions.

The Government having decided that the present constitution and administration of Railways shall be altered, the Bill as introduced, so far as the main principles and broad features are concerned, meets to a considerable extent the views of your Board. There are, however, many details of the Bill —some of them of even critical importance—which will need watchful consideration and careful amendment during the progress of the Bill through Parliament. In regard to such amendments the Companies have reserved to themselves full liberty of action, and if, during the proceedings, difficulty should arise upon any question of substantial importance, which, in the opinion of your Board, makes it desirable for the Proprietors to be consulted, a meeting will be called for the purpose.

Yours faithfully,
C. N. LAWRENCE,
Deputy-Chairman.

Ashton Davies, Divisional General Superintendent of the LNWR Northern Division 1922.
PHOTO COURTESY LANCASHIRE & YORKSHIRE RAILWAY SOCIETY.

Manchester base, from which he now controlled a much more extensive empire, with the old LNWR lines added to those of the LYR.

Other functions, which were not split between Northern and Southern Divisions, were divided along originating Company lines. Division 'A' covered the area of the LNWR pre-amalgamation, with Division 'B' comprising everything LYR.

Watson's article in the January 1922 Gazette stated that:

'The Divisional General Superintendents' Department will include the control and supervision of the whole of the arrangements concerned in the operating or working of the traffic whether conveyed by road, rail or water, including:

a. Passenger Commercial
b. Passenger Operating
c. Goods Train Operating
d. Goods Yard Working
e. Collection and Delivery Arrangements
f. Passenger Train and Goods Train Traffic Station Staff
g. Locomotive Running as hereinafter defined
h. Marine Department
i. Horse Department'

Regarding point g. above, it was stated that:

'The Locomotive Running and Shed Staff on what was formerly the Lancashire and Yorkshire Railway will continue to be administered by the Divisional General Superintendent (Northern) and the Superintendent of Motive Power (Division "A")... will continue to administer that department on the portion of the new London & North Western Railway which he formerly supervised (ie the whole of the pre-amalgamation LNWR).' Curiously, whilst Watson makes no reference here to a corresponding post of Superintendent of Motive Power (Division 'B'), the structure he set out did include such a post, held by F. W. Attock, who had been the LYR's Outside Locomotive Superintendent since 1912 (and who was also the son of Frederick Attock, who had been the LYR's Carriage and Wagon Superintendent 1877-1895).

Regarding other functions controlled and supervised by the Department:

'The District Goods Manager, District Traffic Superintendents, and Irish Traffic Manager, will be responsible to the Divisional General Superintendents...

'Communications respecting matters relating to the working of freight train traffic must, in future, be sent to the Divisional General Superintendents instead of to the Chief Goods Manager.

'The whole of the Traffic Staff (i.e. passenger and goods) at the stations will be under the control of the respective Divisional General Superintendents.'

The Irish Traffic Manager referred to above, who was based at North Wall Station, Dublin, was responsible to the District General Superintendent (Northern), as were the three District Marine Superintendents (based at Holyhead, Fleetwood and Goole).

'The Chief Goods Manager (S. H. Hunt, based at Euston) will control the whole of the commercial arrangement in connection with traffic conveyed by freight trains, including the conditions of the contract under which freight train traffic is to be accepted from the public and the rates to be put into operation in connection therewith. He will have the assistance of two Divisional Goods Managers designated "Divisional Goods Manager (Southern)" and "Divisional Goods Manager (Northern)".'

CHIEF ENGINEER

E. F. C. Trench, who had been the LNWR's Chief Engineer since 1909, retained his Euston base as Chief Engineer of the Company post-amalgamation. He was assisted by Divisional Engineers for 'A' and 'B' Divisions: Messrs Williams (Crewe) and Coomber (Manchester) respectively. The responsibilities of the Chief Engineer were described as follows:

a. The design and execution of all new works within the scope of his department.
b. The maintenance of the permanent way, buildings and any equipment which the General Manager allocates to his department.
c. The provision and maintenance of telephones, telegraphs, block instruments, track circuits and any electrical appliances used in connection with signalling.
d. The provision and maintenance of the lighting arrangements of the railway.'

George Hughes, who became Chief Mechanical and Electrical Engineer of the LNWR following the amalgamation in 1922 (courtesy Lancashire & Yorkshire Railway Society).

CHIEF MECHANICAL AND ELECTRICAL ENGINEER

The LYR's George Hughes became Chief Mechanical and Electrical Engineer, as a result of which the LNWR's H. P. M. Beames was effectively demoted to the post of Divisional Mechanical Engineer (Crewe). The corresponding post of Divisional Mechanical Engineer (Horwich) was held by G. N. Shawcross.

The Chief Mechanical and Electrical Engineer was responsible for:

a. The design, construction and maintenance of all locomotives, with the exception of the work done by the Divisional General Superintendents, and the Superintendent of Motive Power (Division "A"). (Again, there was no reference to the Superintendent of Motive Power (Division 'B')).
b. The design, construction and maintenance of rolling stock.
c. The generation and distribution of electric power (whether for traction or lighting), including the control and supervision of the power houses, sub-stations and all equipment used in connection therewith.
d. The provision and maintenance of all outdoor machinery.

Posts responsible to the Chief Mechanical and Electrical Engineer included:

- Divisional Carriage Superintendent (Wolverton) – A. R. Trevithick
- Divisional Wagon Superintendent (Earlestown) – W. W. H. Warneford
- Divisional Carriage and Wagon Superintendent (Newton Heath) – F. E. Gobey.

OTHER POSTS

The new Company's Land and Estate Agent was J. R. Ball (Euston), with Divisional Land and Estate Agents, together with Divisional Rating Surveyors, being allocated to the Northern and Southern Divisions.

The Company's Accountant was J. F. Gee (Euston) and the Audit Accountant, F. G. Evans (Euston).

Divisional Storekeepers and Divisional Hotel Managers were allocated to Divisions 'A' and 'B'.

INTO THE LMS

There was little time for this structure of the 'new' LNWR to become established, as, just one year later, the Company was absorbed into the LMS. But if the aim of the amalgamation had been to strengthen the hand of the LNWR and put it into a dominant position relative to the Midland, that plan, initially, seemed to have been successful.

The final LNWR Chairman, Charles Lawrence, became the first Chairman of the LMS; R. C. Irwin was its first Secretary; and Arthur Watson was appointed LMS General Manager.

When Watson set out the 'Interim Organisation of the Company' in the first (January 1923) issue of the LM&SR Gazette, there was much that had a familiar look. Even the Gazette itself was essentially unchanged, apart from the updated title, for most of 1923 at least.

The Department of the Chief General Superintendent now comprised three Divisions: Western, Midland and Northern. The Northern Division included all Scottish lines and the Midland Division was essentially the Midland Railway with the addition of the Stratford-upon-Avon and Midland Junction. The Western Division covered the post-amalgamation LNWR, together with the North Staffordshire, Furness, Maryport and Carlisle and Dundalk, Newry & Greenore railways.

The post of General Superintendent (Western Division) went to Ashton Davies (who again kept his office at Hunt's Bank, Manchester), although now he was responsible to Chief General Superintendent J. H. Follows (ex-Midland Railway).

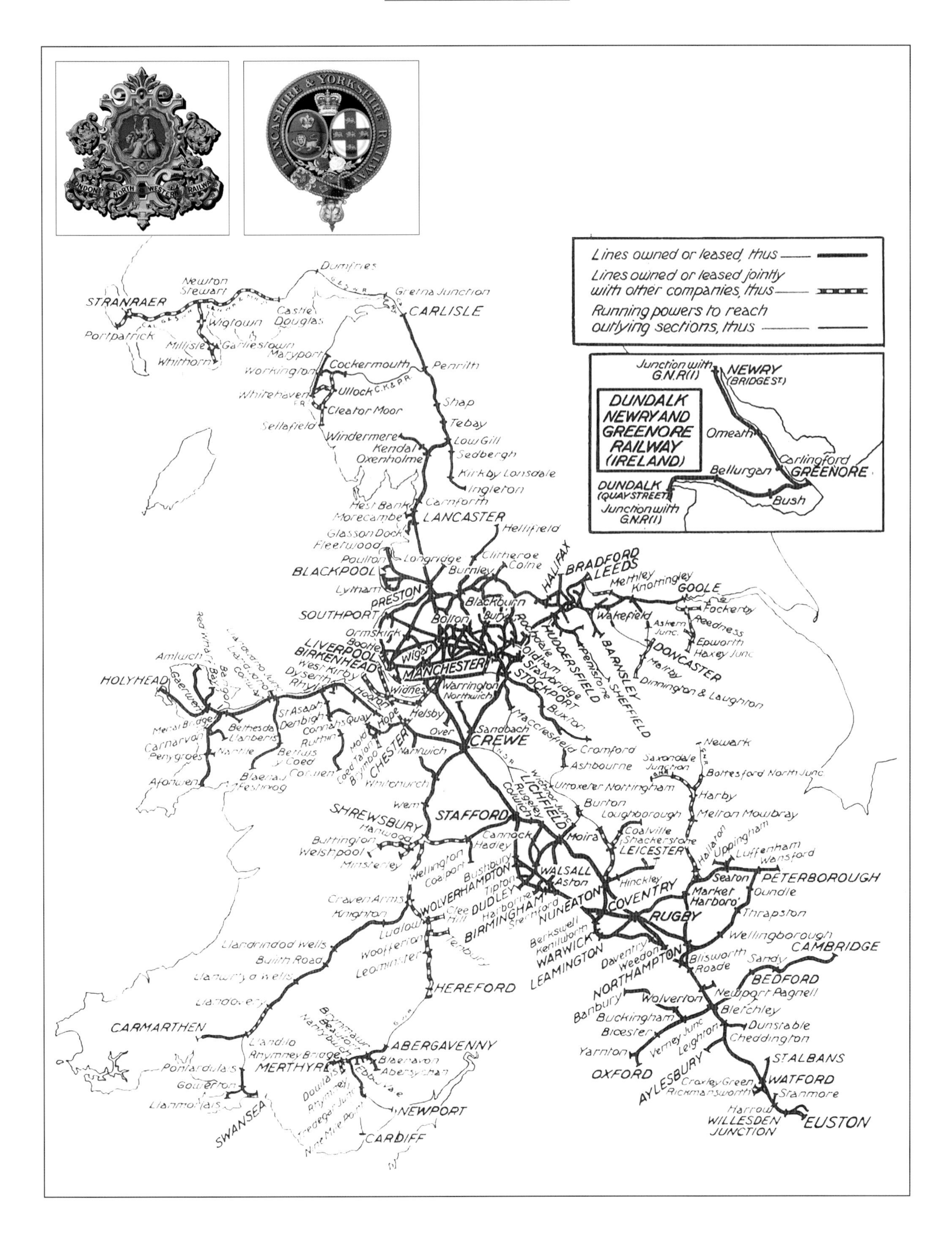
LONDON NORTH WESTERN RAILWAY
LANCASHIRE & YORKSHIRE RAILWAY
Lines owned or leased, thus
Lines owned or leased jointly with other companies, thus
Running powers to reach outlying sections, thus
DUNDALK NEWRY AND GREENORE RAILWAY (IRELAND)
Junction with G.N.R.(I)
NEWRY (BRIDGE ST.)
Omeath
Carlingford
GREENORE
Bellurgan
Bush
DUNDALK (QUAY STREET)
Junction with G.N.R.(I)
Dumfries
Gretna Junction
CARLISLE
Newton Stewart
STRANRAER
Portpatrick
Wigtown
Castle Douglas
Millisle
Garliestown
Whithorn
Maryport
Cockermouth
Workington
Penrith
Whitehaven
Ullock
Cleator Moor
Shap
Tebay
Sellafield
Windermere
Low Gill
Kendal
Sedbergh
Oxenholme
Kirkby Lonsdale
Ingleton
Hest Bank
Carnforth
Morecambe
LANCASTER
Hellifield
Glasson Dock
Fleetwood
Poulton
Longridge
Clitheroe
Colne
BLACKPOOL
Burnley
Lytham
PRESTON
HALIFAX
BRADFORD
LEEDS
Methley
Knottingley
GOOLE
Fockerby
SOUTHPORT
Blackburn
Bolton
Bury
Rochdale
Wakefield
Askern Junc.
Reedness
Epworth
Haxey Junc
Ormskirk
Bootle
LIVERPOOL
BIRKENHEAD
Wigan
MANCHESTER
Oldham
HUDDERSFIELD
Penistone
BARNSLEY
DONCASTER
Maltby
Dinnington & Laughton
SHEFFIELD
Amlwch
HOLYHEAD
West Kirby
Dyserth
Rhyl
Widnes
Warrington
Northwich
Stalybridge
STOCKPORT
Buxton
Hooton
St Asaph
Denbigh
Connah's Quay
Hope
Helsby
Macclesfield
Menai Bridge
Bethesda
Llanberis
Ruthin
Mold
Over
Sandbach
CREWE
Cromford
Carnarvon
Penygroes
Nantlle
Bettws y Coed
Corwen
CHESTER
Nantwich
Ashbourne
Newark
Saxondale Junction
Bottesford North Junc
Afonwen
Blaenau Ffestiniog
Whitchurch
Uttoxeter
Nottingham
Harby
Wem
LICHFIELD
Burton
Loughborough
Melton Mowbray
SHREWSBURY
STAFFORD
Hanwood
Cannock
Moira
Coalville
Shackerstone
Uppingham
Buttington
Hadley
LEICESTER
Hallaton
Luffenham
Wansford
Welshpool
Minsterley
Wellington
Coalport
Bushbury
WALSALL
Aston
Hinckley
Seaton
PETERBOROUGH
Craven Arms
WOLVERHAMPTON
Tipton
DUDLEY
NUNEATON
COVENTRY
Market Harboro'
Oundle
Knighton
Ludlow
Clee Hill
BIRMINGHAM
Harborne
RUGBY
Thrapston
Berkswell
Kenilworth
Wellingborough
Llandrindod Wells
Woofferton
Tenbury
WARWICK
Daventry
CAMBRIDGE
Builth Road
Leominster
LEAMINGTON
Weedon
NORTHAMPTON
Blisworth
Roade
Sandy
BEDFORD
HEREFORD
Banbury
Wolverton
Newport Pagnell
Llandovery
Buckingham
Bletchley
CARMARTHEN
Bicester
Verney Junc
Leighton
Dunstable
Cheddington
Llandilo
ABERGAVENNY
Yarnton
Rhymney Bridge
Blaenavon
Abersychan
ST. ALBANS
Pontardulais
MERTHYR
OXFORD
AYLESBURY
WATFORD
Gowerton
Croxley Green
Rickmansworth
Stanmore
Llanmorlais
NEWPORT
Harrow
SWANSEA
WILLESDEN JUNCTION
EUSTON
CARDIFF

E. F. C. Trench became LMS Chief Engineer and Messrs Williams and Coomber remained in post as 'Divisional Engineer, Permanent Way (present Division "A")' and 'Divisional Engineer (present Division "B")' respectively.

George Hughes (Horwich) became the first LMS Chief Mechanical and Electrical Engineer, with Sir Henry Fowler (ex-Midland) designated Deputy Chief Mechanical Engineer. H. P. M. Beames remained as Mechanical Engineer (Crewe), as did G. N. Shawcross, Mechanical Engineer (Horwich).

Within just a few years, of course, much of this was to change, as ex-Midland men took over the most senior positions. But that, as they say, is another story.

Acknowledgement

We are grateful to Roger Mellor of the Lancashire & Yorkshire Railway Society for making available photographs from that Society's collection.

The new order following amalgamation was demonstrated by this photograph, which appeared on p255 of the September 1922 issue of the L&NWR Gazette, it's caption read: 'Northern Section L.&N.W. Heavy Mineral Train, Engine 0-8-0 No. 246.' The photograph shows a L&YR large-boilered 0-8-0 hauling a typically long train of Yorkshire coal along the LYR's Calder Valley main line at Mytholmroyd. PHOTO: LANCASHIRE & YORKSHIRE RAILWAY SOCIETY, PHOTOGRAPHER F. E. MACKAY.

Another eight-coupled locomotive, this time of L.&N.W. origin in the shape of Bowen-Cooke G2a Class 7F No. 49115 which is passing Nuneaton Up Sidings signal box under the watchful eye of the duty signalman. PHOTO: ARTHUR MACE © THE TRANSPORT TREASURY.

THE LONDON & NORTH WESTERN RAILWAY SOCIETY

REGISTERED CHARITY: L&NWR SOCIETY NO. 1110210

The Society was founded by the late Eric Rayner in 1973 to bring together all who are interested in the LNWR, its constituent companies and associated lines. We have an active Staff History section. Members receive four Journals, four Newsletters and two Modelling Supplements each year, as well as other occasional publications, plus greatly reduced prices on publications that we are associated with. Society events include the Annual Crewe Luncheon,the 'Steam Up' where we visit a Model Engineers' track and members run their live steam LNWR locomotives, and Open Days with illustrated talks on LNWR subjects, displays and sales stands, relics and archives. The Society's forum at www.lnwrs.org.uk hosts a lot of information about 'The Premier Line' and we also have a Facebook Group and a Facebook Page. You'll find both by searching in FB for 'London & North Western Railway Society' Research Facilities. The Society has its own Study Centre at Kenilworth housing an extensive library and collection of archive material (approximately 8,000 documents),photographs (20,000+), plans and drawings (approximately 7,200) and relics. Meetings and Research Days are frequently held there for members. The Centre houses sophisticated equipment for scanning books, drawings and large plans. Working From Home Members do not necessarily have to travel to Kenilworth to do their research or help with archive expansion. We host on computer a Document Management System (DMS) which houses our collection of digital images (photo collection) and all the results of scanning plans and documents.

The number of items we now have digitally available is (approximate figures): 6,900 Drawings, 1,500 Documents, 16,000 Photographs, 815 Books In addition, more are always being processed, and there are nearly 10,000 photographs scanned but yet to be captioned, plus others yet to be scanned from donated or recently acquired purchases.

If we can keep a digital copy of the material, we offer a free scanning service of members' and non-members' items; otherwise rates are extremely competitive. We also have received a large number of duplicate drawing copies. If they are a better copy, we replace the original, and sell the old copy, together with the other duplicates, to raise funds. We often have a large stock to sell, please enquire. Contact: projects@lnwrs.org.uk

Applications for membership may be made online at lnwrs.org.uk or to: The Membership Secretary, 19 Totternhoe Road, Dunstable, Bedfordshire LU6 2AF. Email: membership@lnwrs.org.uk

Two ex-L&NWR Webb Coal Tanks, Nos. 58926 and 58902 are pictured at Abercynon shed in 1954. Both of these Crewe-built locos had working lives of over 70 years – No. 58902 entered service in 1884 as L&NWR No. 796, being renumbered 7710 by the LMS and eventually withdrawn by BR in December 1954. No. 58926 started life in September 1888 as No. 1054, absorbed by the LMS the loco was renumbered No. 7799, but not until March 1926, withdrawn at the end of October 1958 the loco was thankfully saved and is now in the care of the Bahamas Locomotive Society. PHOTO: NEVILLE STEAD © THE TRANSPORT TREASURY

THE RESORT-NAMED PATRIOT 4-6-0s OF THE L.M.S.R.

BY DAVID ANDERSON

LMS Patriot 4-6-0 No. 45520 Llandudno storms past Slaithwaite with a Hull to Liverpool express in March 1951.
Photo: Kenneth Field © Rail Archive Stephenson

Between the introduction of the 'Royal Scot' class 4-6-0s in 1927 and the first of the Stanier Pacifics in 1933, the LMSR built the 'Patriot' or 'Baby Scot' class 4-6-0s at Crewe and Derby works. The first two engines were classified as 1930 rebuilds of the London and North Western Railway 'Claughton' 4-6-0s whilst the remainder of the class were new locomotives to a Henry Fowler design with a total of 52 engines being placed in main line service between 1932 and 1934, 18 of which were rebuilt by Ivatt from 1946.

The 4-6-0s received a variety of names apart from 10 engines which remained nameless although these were allocated titles but not applied. 13 engines of the class were bestowed with the names of popular holiday resorts or destinations served by the LMSR along the North Wales and Lancashire coasts with six of the 'Patriots' carrying the appropriate civic coats-of-arms above the nameplates as shown in the following list.

Throughout this feature, the original LMSR 1934 numbering scheme has been used. All of the engines had 40,000 added to their numbers when taken over by British Railways.

No. 5511 Isle of Man(1)
No. 5514 Holyhead
No. 5515 Caernarvon
No. 5520 Llandudno(2)
No. 5521 Rhyl(2)
No. 5522 Prestatyn
No. 5523 Bangor
No. 5524 Blackpool
No. 5525 Colwyn Bay(2)
No. 5526 Morecambe and Heysham(2)
No. 5527 Southport(2)
No. 5546 Fleetwood
No. 5548 Lytham St. Annes

1. No. 5511 carried the island's crest above the nameplate.
2. At one time, these engines carried the town's civic coat-of-arms above the nameplate.

No. 5511 Isle of Man

Set in the middle of the Irish Sea, the Isle of Man with its capital town of Douglas has an area of 227 square miles which makes it one of the smallest independent sovereign countries under the Crown. The island was annexed by England in the 13th century and is ruled by a Lieutenant Governor appointed by the Crown but with its own Parliament – the Tynwald – which administers its laws and taxes. From the island's highest point of Snaefell (2,034 feet) served by a mountain railway from 1895, England, Scotland and Wales are all within view. In 1873, the first section of a narrow gauge steam railway system centred on Douglas was opened serving Port Erin, Castletown and across to Peel on the west coast before continuing eastwards to Ramsey. With its regular steamer sailings from the mainland, the Isle of Man became a popular holiday destination with main sea-crossings operated by the London and North Western Railway and the LMSR from Liverpool and Fleetwood to Douglas together with seasonal sailings by other pre-Grouping railway companies including services from Silloth to Douglas, Whitehaven to Ramsey, Barrow-in-Furness to Douglas and Ardrossan to Douglas.

No. 5511 *Isle of Man* was built at Crewe Works in August 1932 and carried the first LMSR number 5942. The 'Patriot' 4-6-0 later received an attractive coat-of-arms fitted above the nameplate at a ceremony in 1938, the location not identified. It remained in original condition during its service from a variety of depots including Camden, Bushbury, Crewe North and Willesden before being withdrawn from Carlisle Upperby in February 1961.

No. 5511 Isle of Man is pictured on Bangor shed on 28th March 1948. Almost 70 years on from this photograph one of the nameplates sold for £26,000. © Manchester Locomotive Society/The LMS-Patriot Project.

No. 5514 Holyhead

Situated on Holy Island off the coast of Anglesey, the once important port of Holyhead was the western terminus of the London and North Western Railway, the City of Dublin Steam Packet Company and the LMSR for their cross-channel Irish passenger, freight and mail services to and from Dublin (North Wall), Kingstown (Dun Laoghaire) and to the Irish port of Greenore from the terminus Admiralty Pier. It was also the ultimate destination for the famous Irish Mail railway service from London Euston. Historically, the Chester & Holyhead was an independent railway company formed to link up with the

Both nameplates are appropriately preserved in Holyhead, one in the Public Library, the other in the Town Hall.

NO. 5514 with backing plate but no nameplate pictured at Camden. The engine was named briefly in late 1938 so the picture probably dates from around that time.
PHOTO: WILLIE HERMISTON © THE TRANSPORT TREASURY.

Chester and Crewe Railway and by 1842, a through route was in operation between Euston and Chester with Bangor being reached by rail in 1848, passengers using Telford's suspension bridge over the Menai Straits until the Britannia tubular bridge was completed.

No. 5514 *Holyhead* was built at Crewe Works in September 1932 and was named in 1938 although no official ceremony of the occasion has been recorded. The 'Patriot' was rebuilt in March 1947 and spent most of its working life at Camden and Crewe sheds before being withdrawn from Derby shed in May 1961.

NO. 5515 CAERNARVON

Located overlooking the southern end of the Menai Straits on the former L&NWR and LMSR line between Bangor and Pwllheli, Caernarvon, the resort and ceremonial capital of Wales, is famous for its castle, the foundation stone of which was laid in 1283. In 1969, it was the spectacular setting for the investiture of Prince Charles as Prince of Wales.

The 'Patriot' 4-6-0 carrying the name was delivered from Crewe Works in October 1932 (first LMSR No. 5992, named in 1938) and remained at work in its original form until withdrawal from Manchester Newton Heath depot in June 1962. The name *Caernarvon* was previously allocated to London and North Western Railway 'George V' class 4-4-0 No 984.

NO. 5515 in its previous guise as NO. 5992 pictured at an unknown location in the mid-1930s. PHOTO: © THE TRANSPORT TREASURY.

NO. 5520 LLANDUDNO

One of the resort-named engines to carry the civic coat-of-arms crest above the nameplate. No. 5520 was named in 1937, probably at Llandudno station, but not confirmed. Probably the most popular of all the Welsh coast holiday destinations, the North Shore beach is enclosed by the headlands of Great Orme (679 feet), which is reached by cable operated tramway, and Little Orme (464 feet). Served by the main coastal railway from 1858, the resort is only one and a half hours journey time from Liverpool and two hours from Manchester making it a convenient journey for holidaymakers and city commuters alike. By 1885, the town's population had risen to over 5,000, a figure which had doubled by the turn of the century. Due to the ease of railway communication, it was provided with business trains which included 'club' coaches introduced by the L&NWR from 1908.

The 'Patriot' 4-6-0 which carried the name was one of six engines of the class presented with civic coat-of-arms crests. *Llandudno* was built at Derby Works in 1933, named in 1937 and ran in original condition until withdrawal from Liverpool Edge Hill depot in May 1962.

NO. 5521 RHYL

Sandy beaches and holiday entertainment at Rhyl and its eastern neighbour Prestatyn produced a healthy financial return for the L&NWR and LMSR companies, the railway helping to open up passenger travel along the North Wales coast with extra trains and excursion traffic from the main centres of Lancashire and Yorkshire industry. Visitors could also visit the nearby Rhuddlan Castle, its building begun in 1277, and also a miniature railway engineered by Bassett-Lowke and Henry Greenly.

No. 5521 was also Derby-built in March 1933, was named in 1937 and carried a civic coat-of-arms crest above the nameplate.

LMSR PATRIOT RESORTS AND PORTS

1	Isle of Man	A	Barrow-in-Furness
2	Morecambe and Heysham	B	Lancaster
3	Fleetwood	C	Preston
4	Blackpool	D	Blackburn
5	Lytham St. Annes	E	Wigan
6	Southport	F	Liverpool
7	Prestatyn	G	Birkenhead
8	Rhyl	H	Chester
9	Colwyn Bay	I	Douglas (I.O.M.)
10	Llandudno		
11	Bangor		
12	Holyhead		
13	Caernarvon		

Isle of Man
Lake District
Morecambe Bay
Irish Sea
Liverpool Bay
Anglesey
Holy Island
Menai Straight
Caernarvon Bay

Looking immaculate in original LMS livery, No. 5521 Rhyl prepares to depart Birmingham New Street on 17th May 1938. PHOTO: © EDWARD TALBOT COLLECTION.

Rebuilt in November 1946, the 'Patriot' 4-6-0 was in LMSR and BR service until its withdrawal from Wigan Springs Branch shed in September 1963.

No. 5522 Prestatyn

At the northern end of the 8th century Offa's Dyke, which marked the boundary between England and Wales, is the holiday resort of Prestatyn with its four miles of sandy beaches offering the same visitor facilities as the neighbouring resorts of Rhyl, Colwyn Bay and Llandudno.

One of the Derby-built series of 1933 'Patriot" 4-6-0s, No. 5522 *Prestatyn* received its name in 1939, possibly at Prestatyn station, but this is not confirmed. The engine underwent rebuilding in January 1949 and before its withdrawal from service at Manchester Longsight depot in September 1964, the 4-6-0 was based at Bushbury, Crewe North and Camden.

No. 5523 Bangor

Bangor, the cathedral and university city of North Wales, is situated on the Menai Straits overlooking the Menai Bridge and the Isle of Anglesey, 9 miles to the north east of Caernarvon. The collections at Penrhyn Castle, 2 miles to the east of Bangor, which was completed in 1840, includes the display of early locomotives. Built at Crewe Works in March 1933 as LMSR No. 6026, the 'Patriot' carrying the name *Bangor* was renumbered 5523 in 1934 and finally 45523 by British Railways. The 4-6-0 was named in 1938 and rebuilt in October 1948. Its withdrawal came in January 1964 after main line service at Bushbury, Crewe North, Camden and finally Willesden.

No. 5523 at Leamington Spa Avenue in 1936. PHOTO: GORDON COLTAS TRUST © MANCHESTER LOCOMOTIVE SOCIETY.

NO. 5524 BLACKPOOL

Blackpool began to develop as a recreational resort in the mid-18th century and became busiest during the summer months when the Lancashire and Yorkshire mines, factories and mills closed for the annual 'wakes' or holidays. At first reached by a branch line of the Preston and Wyre railway, its seven mile promenade and three piers are well known for the autumn illuminations, the scene dominated by the 518 feet high Blackpool Tower.

Blackpool's success owes much to the railway and the additional popularity of an extensive electric tramway system. The lines serving Blackpool were jointly owned by the Lancashire and Yorkshire and the London and North Western railways, their termini becoming Blackpool (Talbot Road, later North) and Central. The former station was rebuilt with 15 platforms in 1898 and in 1900, Central station with 14 platforms. By 1903, the original coast line from Lytham was bypassed by a direct line from Kirkham, this allowing a faster running time and a five mile reduction in distance from Preston. In 1919, a total of 413,000 passengers arrived at Blackpool at the height of the summer season and on a Saturday in August 1935, a remarkable number of 467 trains arrived and departed from the resort's two stations. The advent of motor transport affected passenger traffic on the once-important railways with the closure of Central station and the termination of the coast line at Blackpool (South) in 1964. Main line services were concentrated at Blackpool (North) after the closure of the direct line in 1967, the station being rebuilt in 1974.

The 'Patriot' 4-6-0 No. 5524 (originally named *Sir Frederick Harrison*) was renamed *Blackpool* at the town's station on 23rd March 1936 in the presence of Sir Josiah Stamp, the Chairman of the LMSR. The engine was built at Crewe Works in March 1933 and was withdrawn in original condition from Liverpool Edge Hill depot in January 1964.

No. 5524 (later 45524) regularly worked the LMSR's 'Fylde Coast Express' between London Euston and Blackpool in 4 hours 22 minutes, 47 minutes faster than the pre-Grouping company schedule.

NO. 5525 COLWYN BAY

Situated three miles to the east of Llandudno, Colwyn – renamed Colwyn Bay in 1876 – provides the usual holiday resort facilities on the 18 mile stretch of the North Wales shoreline with its coastal towns served by the LMSR and previously the London and North Western Railway. Colwyn Bay has become one of the largest towns to the west of the Merseyside region.

Originally named E. TOOTAL BROADHURST, as seen in this picture, NO. 5525 was renamed COLWYN BAY at the town's station in 1938. PHOTO: © THE TRANSPORT TREASURY.

'Patriot' 4-6-0 No. 5525 *Colwyn Bay* was built at Derby Works in 1933 and originally numbered 5916 and named *E. Tootal Broadhurst*. The engine was officially renamed *Colwyn Bay* at the station during a ceremony on 16th June 1938. One of 18 engines of the class to be rebuilt in 1948, No. 5525 was withdrawn from Llandudno Junction shed as No. 45525 in May 1963.

NO. 5526 MORECAMBE AND HEYSHAM

The nameplate of 45526 as carried by the rebuilt 'Patriot', one of its nameplates is on display at the NRM, York. PHOTO: DAVE HILL. © THE LMS-PATRIOT PROJECT.

Built at Derby Works in March 1933 and later rebuilt in February 1947, this 'resort' 'Patriot' was named at Morecambe station by the Mayor on 6th October 1937, the crest bearing the civic coat-of-arms being added above the nameplate in December of that year. The 'Patriot' 4-6-0 was withdrawn from service at Carlisle Upperby shed in October 1964.

Two old villages were merged to become known as Morecambe and Heysham and grew as popular Lancashire holiday coast resorts. Morecambe station was originally called Poulton-le-Sands and was reached by railway from Lancaster in June 1848.

LMS Patriot 4-6-0 No. 45524 Blackpool and Jubilee 4-6-0 No. 45722 Defence at Hay Fell with a Liverpool to Glasgow express in 1949.

Photo: F. R. Hebron © Rail Archive Stephenson.

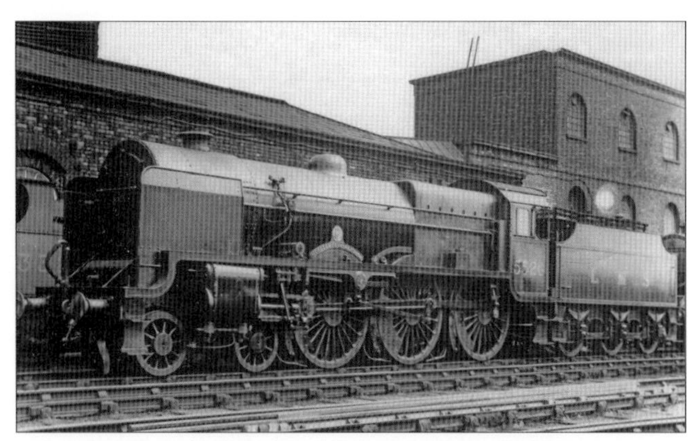

NO. 5526 at Crewe Works on an unknown date. PHOTO: THE LMS-PATRIOT PROJECT © MANCHESTER LOCOMOTIVE SOCIETY.

By 1850, the Midland and L&NWR companies had jointly completed a through route from Leeds and Bradford to Morecambe via Keighley, Skipton and Lancaster and in the early days there was also a direct service from London King's Cross. In 1864, a short branch line was opened to Morecambe from the West Coast main line at Hest Bank and by 1888, the town's stations were renamed Euston Road and Promenade. By 1908, an electric train service was in operation serving Morecambe and Heysham from Lancaster. Railway-owned steamship sailings operated from the developing port of Heysham to Ireland and the Isle of Man.

NO. 5527 SOUTHPORT

Located on the Lancashire coast within easy reach of the city of Liverpool and ten miles from Blackpool, the resort of Southport is well known for its broad, tree-lined mile long Lord Street and its mile long pier railway. The town was reached by the railway on 24th July 1848 from Waterloo, Liverpool, later trains serving Southport from Liverpool Exchange station and a line from Manchester followed in 1855 to the Lancashire and Yorkshire Railway terminus at Chapel Street. The Cheshire Lines Committee also opened a line to a terminus at Lord Street in 1882. Later, many of the lines in the area were electrified. The intricate network of lines around Southport has now been greatly reduced but the town retains its prosperity within striking distance of Liverpool.

NO. 5527 SOUTHPORT pictured at Crewe and waiting a trip to the paint shop. No. 5527 was one of the sixteen of the class to wear the LMS post-war express passenger livery which was black with straw-coloured numerals and letters inset by a thin maroon line, straw and maroon lining, while the first and last boiler bands and the platform angle are painted crimson lake and edged with straw. PHOTO: COURTESY PETE SIKES.

No. 5527 *Southport* was one of the Derby-built series of 'Patriot' 4-6-0s of 1933 and the engine was rebuilt in British Railways days in September 1948. No. 5527 was officially named by the LMSR in 1937 and carried a crest bearing the town's civic coat-of-arms above the nameplates. A Liverpool Edge Hill-based locomotive for most of its existence, No. 5527 was withdrawn from service at Carlisle Kingmoor depot in December 1964.

NO. 5546 FLEETWOOD

One of Britain's chief fishing ports and a holiday and sailing centre, Fleetwood is situated at the mouth of the River Wyre estuary, seven miles north of Blackpool. As with neighbouring coastal towns, its popularity was largely due to the development of the railway which also operated cross-channel steamers from its port to Belfast and the Isle of Man.

'Patriot' No. 5546 *Fleetwood* was one of the final series of engines of the class built at Crewe Works in March 1934 and was named by the LMSR in 1938. The 4-6-0 remained in original condition and was withdrawn from Warrington shed in June 1962.

NO. 5548 LYTHAM ST. ANNES

Built by the LMSR at Crewe Works in May 1934, No. 5548 *Lytham St. Annes* was numerically the last of the resort-named 'Patriots'. The engine was named by the Mayor of the town at the station on 18th December 1937 and was one of six members of the class to receive a civic coat-of-arms crest above the nameplate. No. 5548 remained in original condition during its lifetime and was withdrawn from Nuneaton shed in June 1962.

Situated on the Ribble Estuary between Preston and Blackpool, the town, sometimes spelled as Lytham St. Anne's, is another of the popular holiday destinations at one time served by the LMSR and is also well-known for its championship golf courses, especially Royal Lytham St. Annes.

This article first appeared in issue 33 (May 2017) of The Warrior, the newsletter of The LMS-Patriot Project. To find out more about the project go to: www.lms-patriot.co.uk

NO. 5546 FLEETWOOD departs from Trent Junction station on an unrecorded date.
PHOTO: R. K. BLENCOWE © MANCHESTER LOCOMOTIVE SOCIETY.

NO. 45548 LYTHAM ST. ANNES on shunting duties at Wigston, Leicester on 28th August 1961.
PHOTO: © THE TRANSPORT TREASURY.

PERSONAL RECOLLECTIONS OF CORONATION PACIFICS

PETER TATLOW, PRESIDENT OF THE LMS SOCIETY

(ILLUSTRATIONS BY AUTHOR, UNLESS OTHERWISE INDICATED)

STANIER CLASS 8P 4-6-2 NO. 46231 DUCHESS OF ATHOLL AT SHAP ON 3RD APRIL 1956.
PHOTO: NEVILLE STEAD COLLECTION © THE TRANSPORT TREASURY

Whilst I have no specific recollection of seeing a streamlined 'Coronation' Pacific in all its glory, it is entirely possible, if not probable, that I could have seen one or more in both blue and red liveries, together with their more conventionally styled half-sisters in crimson lake. At the age of just four, my mother and grandmother took my younger brother and me away from the Blitz on 10th September 1940, by removing us from leafy Surrey to the Isle of Bute in the Firth of Clyde. A year and a half later on our return, in May 1942, upon arrival at Euston I definitely remember asking to be able to go and see the engine, but Dad, who had met the train was keen to whisk us across London by taxi to Waterloo station and back to the suburbs before it got dark. I nonetheless recall the streamlined outline of a grimy locomotive, whose livery was probably indistinguishable other than at very close quarters.

For all the hype about streamliners, however, what an inspired choice Hornby made when they selected the non-streamlined version in the form of No. 6231 *Duchess of Atholl* for the LMS express locomotive in their Hornby-Dublo range just before the war. Yes, I know some of those slightly older than me prefer the Princess Royals in gauge O, but they're just showing their age. During the war, I was given a carefully hoarded train set of a clockwork LNER A4 *Sir Nigel Gresley* and twin-articulated teak coaches, which probably accounts from my suffering from schizophrenia to this day! My father, however, had a copy of Edward Beal's book 'Scale Railway Modelling Today', published by A&C Black in 1939. To give my mother some peace, in an era before child care facilities, we two boys were obliged to have an hour's rest every afternoon in an age which these days would probably send a child psychologist into hysterics. Anyway, to while away the time, I would take Beal's book to look through and often paused at the illustration of *Duchess of Atholl*, with single chimney, immediately above one of a pair of A4s and the 0-6-2 tank engine that appeared in guise of all four railway companies.

Once Meccano got re-established after the war, by Christmas 1947 sets of the 3-rail 0-6-2T became available again, but it was to be the following Christmas before I received the long wished for red 4-6-2 locomotive, now with double chimney, to join the Southern tank engine from the previous year, but no coaches. The lack of the latter led to a frustrating time trying to create a pair of crimson lake coach bodies of cardboard painted with water colour on the LNER underframes, but I was always a set of bogies short!

Plate 1:
Hornby Dublo's pre-war 3-rail version of LMS NO. 6231 DUCHESS OF ATHOLL as illustrated in Edward Beal's book.

Plate 2: LMS NO. 6231 DUCHESS OF ATHOLL in real life near Crewe before the war with the Saturdays Only first portion of the 'Mid-Day Scot' made up of the Coronation train set of blue coaches strengthened by additional coaches. PHOTO: N. E. STEAD

I began to wonder after a while, why the tops of the tender front and rear fender plates projected above the line of the loco's cab and I believe I even took a pair of tin snips and trimmed them down. A little later, when 2-rail operation became the thing, on considering the Duchess for conversion, I realised that Hornby, as they often did to allow for the overscale flanges, had compromised on the wheel diameter at 6 feet, instead of 6ft 9in. It then became apparent that in doing so they had failed to lower the axle centres in the chassis, as we then called the frames, to compensate for the reduction in wheel diameter, which meant the whole locomotive sat too low. During conversion to 2-rail, the fitting of the correct diameter wheels immediately restored the locomotive's proper composure.

Although during the latter part of the war I had been able, during occasional visits to my grandparents at Bushey, to watch the string of trains heading to and from London, no doubt including LMS Pacifics of all types, it was a school Boy Scout camp at Martindale in the Lake District that really brought these thoroughbreds to my attention again in July 1953. By now all the streamliners had been de-frocked while most still maintained their shaved off smokeboxes. Many of these and their more conventionally clad half-sisters were still in the BR blue livery and only a few were yet masquerading in GW green! This was also the occasion of the taking of my first railway photograph, the second exposure being none other than No. 46228 *Duchess of Rutland*, as we stood on the platform at Penrith to catch the train

Plate 3: BR NO. 46228 DUCHESS OF RUTLAND in blue livery runs into Penrith with an Up express on 1st August 1953, the author's second ever railway photograph.

home. Being largely a boarding school, most of the boys either used other trains or had left the London train by Crewe. Up to this point the journey had been rather a dawdle and at Crewe a coach with defective draw gear, or was it a through coach for the West Country, was removed and shunted clear. I distinctly recall the ladder on the back of the tender, indicative of a 'one time' streamliner, as the engine reversed up to its train again. Perhaps we also changed footplate crews, because we now set about trying to recover time over track that I do not think was fully restored from the ravages of a lack of maintenance during the war. I certainly remember watching the water in the toilet washbasin swinging from side to side as we raced south. Also to be seen that sunny Saturday afternoon were lineside photographers plying their trade. Drifting down from Primrose Hill Tunnel, we passed Camden shed with the lines of half a dozen or more of these wonderful beasts in several liveries being prepared for their next turn of duty with an express from Euston. One consequence was that my Hornby Dublo Duchess got repainted in Caledonian blue, unlined of course, but then neither had the red one been lined.

Further pursuit of railway photography, however, had to wait for the acquisition of a 35mm camera, the completion of military service and my start of work on the railways in 1957. Having been issued with a photographer's lineside walking permit for my own

Plate 4: The author's Hornby Dublo DUCHESS OF ATHOLL repainted by him in BR blue.

Region, the Southern, it was then an easy matter to obtain the same on other regions. On the London Midland I was initially allowed to walk the line from Watford Tunnel North Portal to Cheddington, together with a similar length on the Midland main line. In this way I was able to photograph trains running into and out of London, including LMS Pacifics. By this time many of them had been decked out in crimson lake again.

There is something about the technical achievement of their design, construction and performance that makes me hanker after a model of *Duchess of Atholl*. Her Grace may have had her home at Blair Atholl in the Highlands, but I really have no excuse for a Coronation Pacific at Inverness in my stated modelling period of between 1928 and 1934!

Plate 5: BR NO. 46229 DUCHESS OF HAMILTON in defrocked state and replacement smokebox on 28th February 1959 with the Up MANXMAN between Cheddington and Tring Cutting Signal Box.

Plate 6: Details and dimensions of both streamlined and non-streamlined versions from the September 1938 edition of Railway Gazette

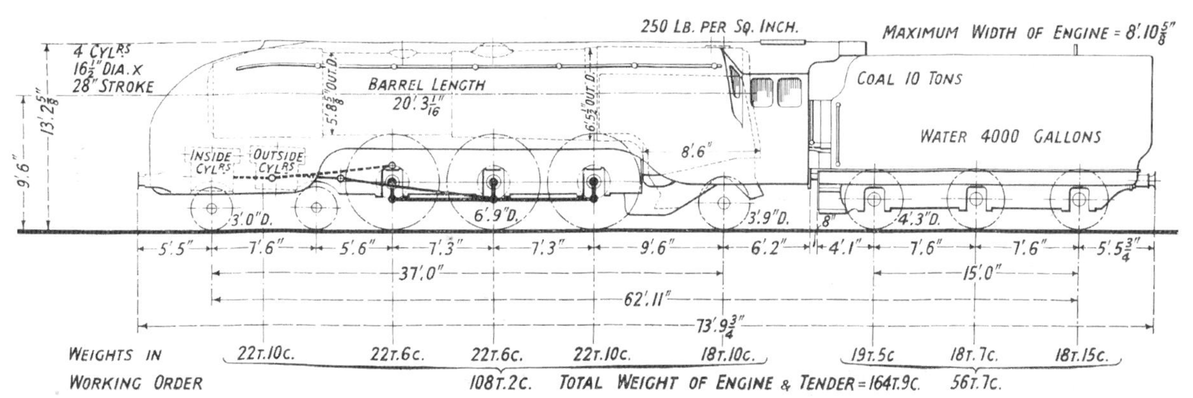

Stanier L.M.S.R. streamlined 4-6-2 of the "Duchess" series, built at Crewe this year

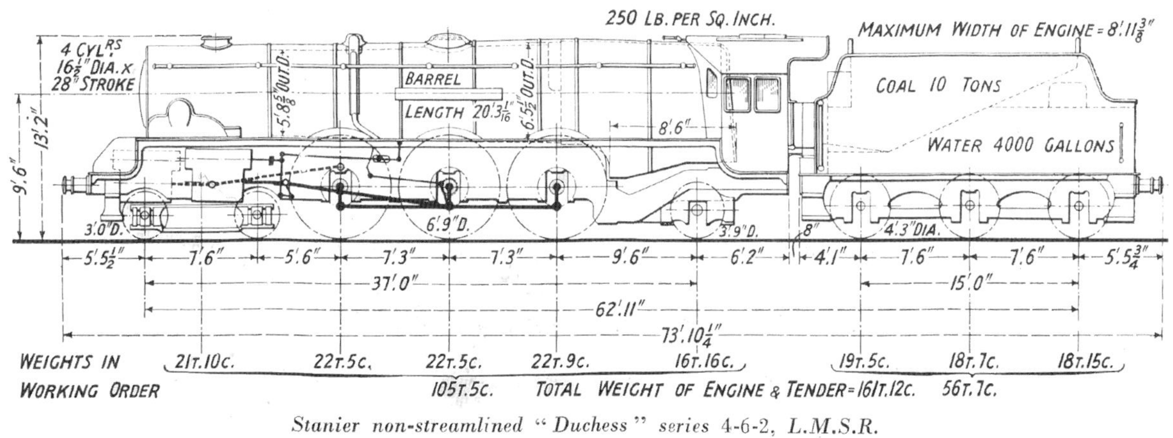

Stanier non-streamlined "Duchess" series 4-6-2, L.M.S.R.

40663 at FORRES – SLS SCOTTISH RAILTOUR 1960

14TH JUNE 1960: Ex-LMS Class 2P 4-4-0 No. 40663, looking immaculate in BR black lined livery, stands at Forres station while working an SLS Scottish Railtour with preserved ex-Caledonian Railway coaches among the consist. This was part of a tour that began at Edinburgh Waverley on 12th June, finishing at Glasgow Central High Level on 17th June 1960. PHOTO: JOHN TOLSON © THE TRANSPORT TREASURY

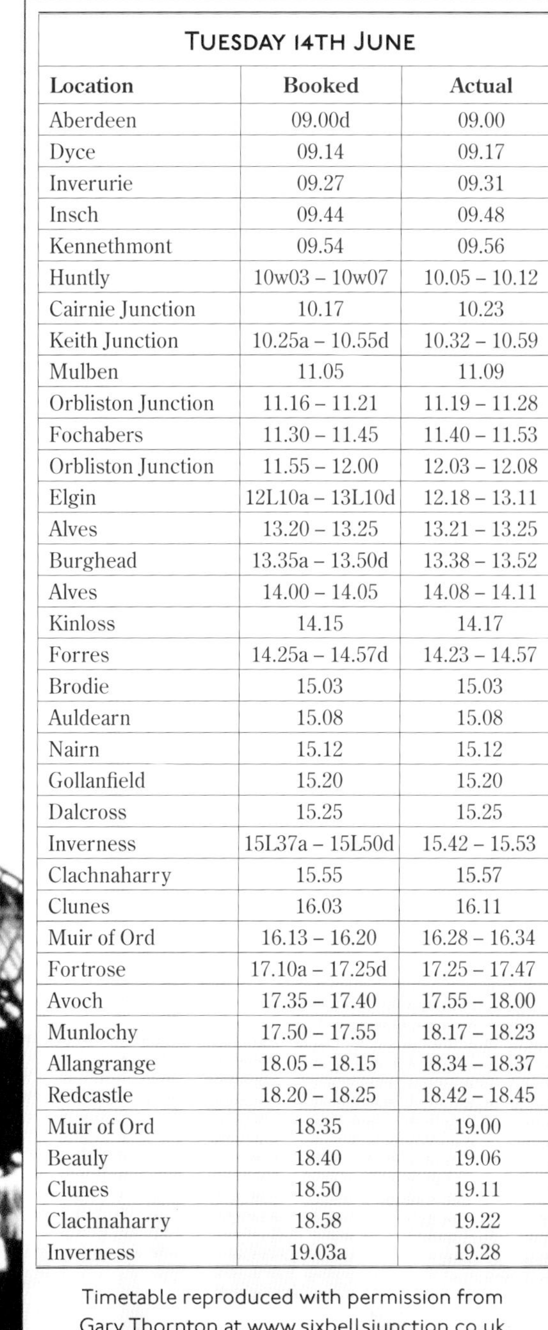

TUESDAY 14TH JUNE		
Location	**Booked**	**Actual**
Aberdeen	09.00d	09.00
Dyce	09.14	09.17
Inverurie	09.27	09.31
Insch	09.44	09.48
Kennethmont	09.54	09.56
Huntly	10w03 – 10w07	10.05 – 10.12
Cairnie Junction	10.17	10.23
Keith Junction	10.25a – 10.55d	10.32 – 10.59
Mulben	11.05	11.09
Orbliston Junction	11.16 – 11.21	11.19 – 11.28
Fochabers	11.30 – 11.45	11.40 – 11.53
Orbliston Junction	11.55 – 12.00	12.03 – 12.08
Elgin	12L10a – 13L10d	12.18 – 13.11
Alves	13.20 – 13.25	13.21 – 13.25
Burghead	13.35a – 13.50d	13.38 – 13.52
Alves	14.00 – 14.05	14.08 – 14.11
Kinloss	14.15	14.17
Forres	14.25a – 14.57d	14.23 – 14.57
Brodie	15.03	15.03
Auldearn	15.08	15.08
Nairn	15.12	15.12
Gollanfield	15.20	15.20
Dalcross	15.25	15.25
Inverness	15L37a – 15L50d	15.42 – 15.53
Clachnaharry	15.55	15.57
Clunes	16.03	16.11
Muir of Ord	16.13 – 16.20	16.28 – 16.34
Fortrose	17.10a – 17.25d	17.25 – 17.47
Avoch	17.35 – 17.40	17.55 – 18.00
Munlochy	17.50 – 17.55	18.17 – 18.23
Allangrange	18.05 – 18.15	18.34 – 18.37
Redcastle	18.20 – 18.25	18.42 – 18.45
Muir of Ord	18.35	19.00
Beauly	18.40	19.06
Clunes	18.50	19.11
Clachnaharry	18.58	19.22
Inverness	19.03a	19.28

Timetable reproduced with permission from Gary Thornton at www.sixbellsjunction.co.uk

THE CALLANDER AND OBAN RAILWAY

BY IAN LAMB

24TH SEPTEMBER 1956: For the first outing of the TV train to Oban, it appeared at the station in two portions, each headed respectively by a 'Black Five'4-6-0 locomotive, Nos. 44908 and 44956, ready to depart for Glasgow (Buchanan Street). In the event No. 44908 slipped to a stand on Glencruitten Bank, and had to be supported to the summit by another 'Black Five' No. 44967, which had been taken off a freight train. During the afternoon two public showings had been held in the trains, proving to be very popular as Oban had no television reception at the time. PHOTO: W. A. C. SMITH

During the railway mania of 1845 speculative Scottish schemes proliferated, but none came to fruition until 1865 when the 'Callander & Oban Railway Act' was authorised. This created a link with the existing 'Dunblane, Doune & Callander' line that had reached Stirling over the tracks of the 'Scottish Central' (later the 'Caledonian Railway').

At 8.15am on Saturday 11th August 1894, the first train pulled out of Glasgow (Queen Street) station, a 'red letter' day in the history of Scottish railway history; the inauguration of the 'West Highland Railway' route northwards. That title encompasses all these routes today, including what is left of the one-time 'Caledonian & Oban Railway'.

This new route reached Killin (Glenoglehead) in 1870; Tyndrum in 1873; Dalmally in 1877, and Oban in 1880, being worked by the 'Caledonian Railway', yet nominally independent until 1923 when it became part of the 'LMS' empire. The Killin branch was opened in 1903.

Precarious financial conditions following the First World War necessitated the Government of the day to establish all the railways coming together under four large companies in 1923, of which the 'Callander & Oban' found itself under the 'LMS' mantle.

The inter-war years saw an imaginative campaign by the 'big four' to regain lost traffic. Innovations included cheap day and evening fares, restaurant cars, Sunday excursions, circular tours and camping coaches, augmented during the British Railways era with 'Television Trains', observation cars, and the diesel 'Six Lochs Land Cruise'.

Personally, I'm sure such initiatives would be supported by the general public today. Indeed, W. A. C. Smith describes the opportunity much more eloquently than I do! "Such initiatives are sadly lacking on today's Scotrail. However, to sell travel by noisy, draughty, outdated diesel multiple units cluttered with backpackers and their impediments, and with viewing of the often spectacular scenery severely restricted by the uncontrolled growth of lineside vegetation, is undoubtedly beset with difficulties. The holding out of the begging bowl to be filled by an indulgent taxpayer is an ever so much easier option."

Dr. Beeching's 1963 report into the reshaping of the nationalised British Railways recommended closing half of the existing 17,000 miles of track plus 2,000 stations, and phasing out steam traction. That report resulted in removal of the 'Callander & Oban" line between Dunblane and Crianlarich, including the Killin branch in 1965, resulting in Oban trains being diverted to Glasgow over

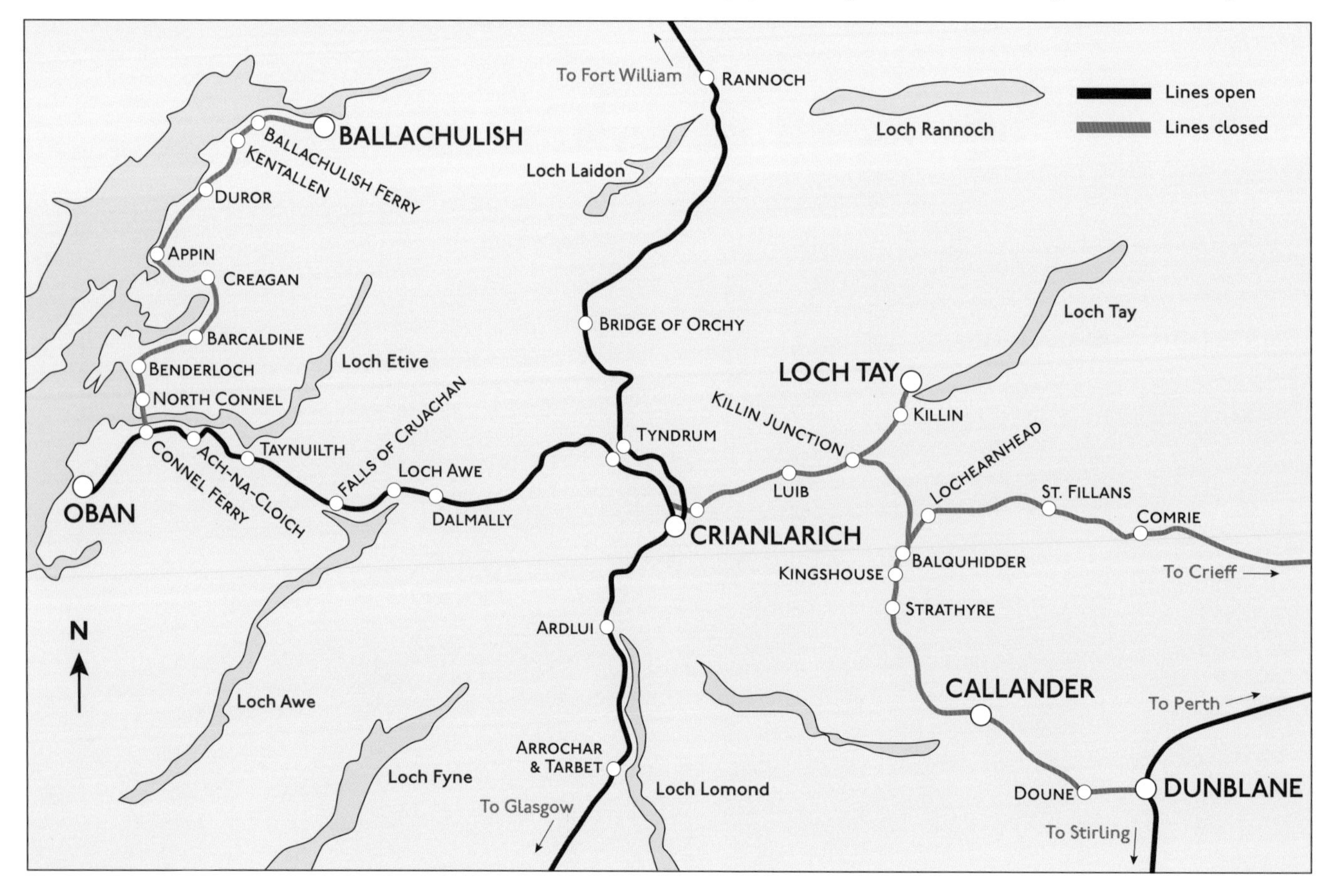

20TH JUNE 1959: Strange bedfellows Class 'K2' 2-6-0 No. 61786 and Class 'B1' 4-6-0 No. 61261 on the connecting spur linking the low level 'Callander & Oban' line with that of the 'NBR' 'West Highland' upper at Crianlarich with the 1.45pm Television Train excursion from Glasgow Buchanan Street, returning to Queen Street. PHOTO: W. A. C. SMITH

18TH JUNE 1962: The Killin branch train service originally ended at the Loch Tay station to connect with steamer services on the loch, but the last mile of track was closed to passengers at the outbreak of war in 1939. It continued to be used by the branch locomotive where its small lochside engine shed was located. As can be seen, the station building survived as a private residence. BR Standard 2-6-4T No. 80092 is about to restart its 'Scottish Tour' special train for railway enthusiasts from 'South of the Border'. PHOTO: W. A. C. SMITH

the 'West Highland' line at Crianlarich. The Ballachulish branch was abandoned in the spring of 1966.

During 1962 steam locomotives were replaced by diesels on these lines, with the exception of Killin and a few Stirling to Callander workings. When the Killin branch was closed prematurely on Monday 27th September 1965, together with the railway from Callander to Crianlarich because of a rockfall in Glen Ogle, the locomotive in use was BR Standard 2-6-4T No. 80093. The Dunblane to Callander section was closed as planned on Monday 1st November 1965. On that occasion the last steam train was the 5.50pm from Glasgow (Buchanan Street) to Callander on Saturday 30th October, worked by Stanier 'Black Five' 4-6-0 No. 45396, a one-time resident of (63B) Stirling MPD.

Most railway ventures of this kind tend to start from the major cities, but on Saturday 9th July 1960 I chose to commence my journey south from the outpost of Ballachulish Ferry on the south shore at the narrows of Loch Leven in the Scottish Western Highlands.

Time was spent awaiting the ferry crossing, but I soon climbed up through the rhododendron foliage to emerge on to the narrow and gravelly platform to await the local train for Connel Ferry.

Soon the ex-Caledonian 0-4-4 tank locomotive No. 55173 came into view, minutes after its beat had first been heard far down the valley. These marvellous little tank engines always seemed to be so much a part of a Highland branch line and scenery. This day was no exception, and the three-coach suburban train crawled into the station before a rather large crowd at this out-of-the-way halt squashed themselves into any available seating.

Continuing on the 1 in 70 incline, the little loco did its best with this rather heavy load, thundering uphill beneath the flanks of Beinn Bheither and high above the Firth of Lorn. The crescendo noise of the engine's exhaust only added to the significance of it all, whilst a great pall of smoke hung over the landscape on approach to Kentallen a few minutes ahead of time.

This remarkable – but uneconomic – line threaded its way above the sea and loch shores onwards to Duror and Appin. For the moment, this 'Caley' tank engine hissed and panted at Kentallen station waiting for the eastbound Ballachulish train to clear the line some five minutes late. Tablets were exchanged; then we were off!

Keeping a steady 45mph along this leisurely route soon took us past the ruins of Castle Stalker at Appin where this tragic

26TH MAY 1958: McIntosh's ex-Caledonian Railway Class '439' or 'Standard Passenger' 0-4-4T No 55208 at Ballachulish Ferry station, heads the 3.48pm local train from Ballachulish to Oban via Connel Ferry. PHOTO: W. A. C. SMITH

SATURDAY 9th JULY, 1960 CLASS 2P 0-4-4T No. 55173	Timetable	Actual time
Ballachulish Ferry (depart)	10.51	
Kentallen	11.00	
Duror	11.10	
Appin	11.23	
Creagan	11.30	
Benderloch	11.46	
North Connel	–	
Connel Ferry (arrive)	11.55	
'BLACK FIVE' 4-6-0 No. 44880 + Unrecorded sister loco		
Connel Ferry (depart)	12.03	
Oban (arrive)	12.28	
'BLACK FIVE' 4-6-0 No. 45499 + STANDARD 5MT 4-6-0 No. 73151 (as far as Stirling)		
Oban (depart)	17.15	17.25
Connel Ferry (arrive)	17.31	17.43
Ach na Cloich	17.42	17.48
Taynuilt	17.53	17.55
Loch Awe	18.11	18.21
Dalmally	18.17	18.26
Tyndrum (Lower)	18.42	18.50
Crianlarich (Lower)	18.53	19.00
Luib	19.04	19.10
Killin Junction	19.13	19.18
Balquhidder	19.45	19.49
Strathyre	19.52	19.56
Callander	20.08	20.10
Onich	–	–
Doune	20.21	20.24
Dunblane	20.29	20.31
Bridge of Allan	20.34	20.36
Stirling (arrive)	20.40	
Stirling (depart)	21.00	
Larbert	21.13	
Falkirk (Grahamston)	21.20	
Polmont	21.25	
Edinburgh (Princes Street)	21.56	

edifice guards the entrance to Loch Laich. Appin station platform lies on a summit 1 in 600 up, and 1 in 300 down. This location was reached only three minutes behind time, which was good going considering the late departure from Kentallen.

These silver metals turned sharp left in company with the road to take advantage of the Strath of Appin to Creagan, rather than round the coast by Port Appin. Now four minutes late at Creagan, the train headed towards a sharp right curve leading on to a double-girder bridge whose stone piers and abutments over the narrows of Loch Creran stand sentinel like a castle. This bridge saves quite a few miles on the long road journey round the loch's shoreline.

Barcaldine Halt was reached at 11.40am, and then across country from Ferlochan to Benderloch. Gradients were pretty steady here, with Benderloch on a 1 in 400 descending slope westwards above Ardmuckuish Bay. Still four minutes behind time! The railway now ran parallel with the coast before emerging near an apparently derelict airfield at North Connel.

The 27¾ miles Ballachulish branch diverged from the Oban line 6¼ miles out at Connel Ferry, providing four trains daily (five on Saturday; none on Sunday). One service started from the junction station at Connel, whilst the others were through trains from Oban, including two school trains.

Soon, through and across the magnificent cantilever structure of the Connel Ferry Bridge, the small trainload coasted into the station platform still four minutes late. The double-headed Oban train continued the lateness trend by arriving some six minutes behind schedule, and departing a further three minutes later before edging the coast, and then sharply turning inland for the descent to the terminus at Oban.

The two Stanier 4-6-0 locomotives were coupled in the unusual position of boiler to boiler, and on the short remaining journey to the sea, there were stops at the 40mph and 20mph speed limit signs. In particular, the latter stop lasted four minutes, and at its height the train reached 50mph on the descent of the Glencruitten bank towards Oban.

One more stop – of two minutes duration – was made near the signal gantry at Oban Junction to unhitch St Rollox (65B) 'Black 5' No. 44880 from the front of the train. Arrival in Oban was 1232pm – four minutes late – having made up five minutes time from Connel Ferry. Nevertheless, with all the stopping and starting, it made a farce of the timetabled schedule over this short section of track.

On departure from Oban at 5.25pm I reckoned that I should be home by 10.30 at the latest. This train was double-headed by

19TH JULY 1954: Ballachulish station for Glencoe and Kinlochleven (as the branch terminus was officially known) lay in the shadow of the famous slate quarries. 'Caley' Class '439' 0-4-4T No. 55195 prepares to leave with the 3.55pm train for Oban. PHOTO: W. A. C. SMITH

14TH MAY 1960: The Connel Ferry Bridge was a notable engineering feature on the Ballachulish branch, and carried the railway plus a single-track roadway – on which a toll was levied – across the Falls of Lora at the mouth of Loch Etive. 'Caley' Class 2P '439' 0-4-4T comes off the bridge with the 3.47pm train from Ballachulish. PHOTO: W. A. C. SMITH

Stanier 'Black Five' No. 45499 and BR Standard No. 73151 at the front (both engines being Glasgow St Rollox (65B) based) and tailing an observation car at the rear. The ten minutes delay from the scheduled time was caused through awaiting the arrival of an extra train from the south. Once it cleared the single line section we were off!

The two 4-6-0s took the nine coach train (plus observation coach) steadily up the Glencruittem incline at 25mph. On clearing the suburbs of this Highland town, the railway soon threaded its way through purple-heathered hillsides. After topping the summit, speed was soon doubled to 50mph, and retained this mileage per hour until Connel Ferry. Here the train decreased speed rapidly before sauntering into the station only eight minutes late, having gained two for good measure on the ascent.

Loch Etive lay dazzling in the evening sun surrounded by high and steep mountains, some of which were thickly forested. Three more minutes were gained by Auchnacloich, and a further four by Taynuilt; Pass of Brander, Loch Awe and Kilchurn Castle were now prominent in the foreground.

The acceleration of these locomotives from zero to an average 50mph was quite amazing, matched only by their deceleration when called upon, especially bearing in mind that the train was well laden with passengers. No doubt trying to make up lost time, but nevertheless quite an achievement.

Between Taynuilt and Loch Awe the glaciated steep defile forces the road and railway to be almost on top of each other beneath the towering Ben Cruachan (3,689 feet high). The incline took its toll, and once more the train fell behind time, just crawling down to Loch Awe station after passing the derelict Falls of Cruachan station.

Almost immediately beyond Kilchurn Castle and east Loch Awe the line turns sharply over a five-arched, straight-girdered, low-lying viaduct crossing the River Strae before accelerating towards Dalmally and Tyndrum with a nine minutes late arrival. Between these two small townships there is a marvellous view of Glen Orchy. Ben Lui (3,768 feet "The Queen of Scottish Mountains") – at the periphery of the Grampians – towers high to the right whilst the broad but shallow River Lochy threads slowly on its way to Loch Awe.

The source of the mighty River Tay is said to take birth at the far side of Ben Lui, towards Strathfillan. Also at the foot of this mountain is little Lochan na Bi, situated westwards on approach to Tyndrum Lower station, arriving there eight minutes late. On the far side of the valley the 'West Highland' line to Fort William was seen high up on the hillside.

Soon Crianlarich East junction was reached before going under the 'West Highland Railway' viaduct at Crianlarich, with a minute's gain on time! A steady climb was now made above the southern shores of Loch Dochart. Electricity pylons now caught the eye beneath the conical shape of mighty Ben More (3,852 feet). Gradually Loch Dochart and the adjacent Loch I Lubnair receded into the background, and on ascending higher and higher towards Killin Junction, the mountainous ridges around Ben Lawers (3,984 feet) soon came into view.

Another minute had been gained at Luib plus one more at Killin Junction so only being five minutes behind schedule. 'Caley' Class '2P' 0-4-4 tank No. 55263 of 1925 origin stood with its one coach suburban train in the adjacent platform awaiting eventual departure to Killin on the shores of Loch Tay.

Continuing the steep ascent towards Glenoglehead only enhanced the superb views on both sides of the summit, especially

Awe (or Orchy) Viaduct. The impressive double-triangular iron lattice truss viaduct built in 1878–79 on the Callander & Oban Railway crossing the Orchy at the head of Loch Awe two miles west of Dalmally. It is the longest viaduct on the line and has seven spans of 63ft supported on short masonry piers and abutments.

12TH AUGUST 1961: Stanier 4-6-0 No. 45214 skirts Loch Lubnaig with the 12.45pm summer Saturday's train for Oban to Edinburgh (Princes Street). During the winter period the through coaches from Oban to Edinburgh were conveyed to Stirling by the Glasgow bound train. Note the immaculate condition of the track.
PHOTO: W. A. C. SMITH

14TH MAY 1960: Preserved 'Great North of Scotland Railway' 4-4-0 NO. 49 GORDON HIGHLANDER with a Glasgow University special originating at Glasgow (Queen Street), and seen here returning south to Buchanan Street through the Pass of Brander, with the fjord-like end of Loch Awe in the background. The train is passing one of the automatic stone signals which went to danger if a boulder from the steep hillside fell and broke the lineside fencing to land on the track. PHOTO: W. A. C. SMITH

the respective Lochs Tay and Earn. A ten minute halt was made at Glenoglehead – at 941 feet, it was the highest point on the 'Callander & Oban Railway' – to permit the twelve minutes late running 5.15pm train from Glasgow (Buchanan Street) to Oban to clear the loop and allow us to coast down the glen to Balquhidder. Undoubtedly the view above Lochearnhead is rightfully considered to be one of the finest scenes from a railway train anywhere in Britain. Far below, Loch Earn glistened in the sun.

For all the delay at Glenoglehead, the Glasgow bound service was only four minutes late at Balquhidder, so one assumes the passing point at the summit is the regular meeting place for these trains. Ben Vorlich (3,224 feet) overlooks Balquhidder at Kingshouse platform, and soon – still some four minutes late – this train stopped at the beautiful setting of Strathyre.

Loch Lubnaig bisects the road and railway for almost six miles before joining again at the Pass of Leny. Stank Glen on the slopes of Ben Ledi (2,873 feet) is not really an appropriate description of this very attractive and picturesque part of Perthshire. The River Leny was crossed by two individual crescent-shaped, latticed girdered bridges a few hundred yards apart, before diverging under the road on approach to Callander. Only two minutes late at that magnificent station complex.

Doune was quickly reached (three minutes late) followed by Dunblane (two minutes late), and then on the descent (1 in 75) on the Perth-Glasgow main line to Bridge of Allan, before skirting the Wallace Monument and Stirling Castle on approach to the station. Soon leading locos 45499 and 73151 ran across the 'other' Forth Bridge, then tore past the former LNER MPD at Shore Road to arrive at platform 3 only one minute behind time.

On the face of it this seemed a good performance, and yet, the 87 miles from Oban had only yielded an average speed of 27 mph! Nevertheless, it was a very enjoyable run through quite spectacular scenery. Bang on time at 9pm, the Edinburgh connection headed out on its journey from Stirling. Time to 'cop' five locomotives at the engine shed (56343, 57246, 55222, 73107 and 45366) as the train ran past, steadily accelerating towards Larbert.

On the section to Falkirk (Grahamston) there were signs of engineering activities everywhere in the failing light! Electricity pylons threaded their way across the plain to

18TH JUNE 1960: On a fine sunny evening, Stanier 'Black Five' 4-6-0 No. 45125 approaches Killin Junction station with the 5.15pm train from Glasgow (Buchanan Street) to Oban. The five miles Killin branch drops left on a ruling gradient of 1 in 50 behind the signal box. PHOTO: W. A. C. SMITH

Grangemouth, telephone cables from building to building, factories abounded, and a myriad of railway tracks criss-crossed along the way. All in all, quite a dramatic difference to the landscape viewed elsewhere en-route to Stirling.

In no time at all the train took the incline in its stride past Callander Park to join the main 'NBR' Glasgow-Edinburgh metals at the throat of Polmont station. The rest of the journey to Princes Street station was straightforward and uneventful.

1930: Stirling station sees a double-headed arrival in the 1930s, with ex-Caledonian Railway Class 900 4-4-0 No. 14342 as the pilot. The McIntosh designed loco was built at St. Rollox Works and entered service in September 1900 being in service for 39 years until withdrawal in March 1939. The train engine is an unidentified 4-4-0 ex-Midland Compound.
PHOTO: GEORGE C. BETT © TRANSPORT TREASURY.

Another view at Stirling, this time of Drummond Class 2F 0-6-0 (Caledonian Class 294 'Jumbo') No. 57252 passing through light engine, possibly on station pilot duties. Following a competition, the current station buildings were constructed by the Caledonian Railway in 1912-15 by James Miller and William A. Paterson, costing over £35,000 replacing the original 1848 structure. Miller's station building design continued the circular spaces and flowing curves of his celebrated Wemyss Bay station. PHOTO: © TRANSPORT TREASURY.

12TH AUGUST 1961: With a good head of steam for the 1 in 60 climb to Glenoglehead, 'Black Five' 4-6-0 No. 45496 passes Strathyre with the 11.50am express from Glasgow (Buchanan Street) to Oban. This formed a relief train to the regular midday service in the days when workers were restricted to a two-week annual summer holiday, and travelled in large numbers – particularly at seasonal weekends – to attractive destinations. PHOTO: W. A. C. SMITH

12TH MAY 1962: Preserved engines, Caledonian Railway 4-2-2 NO. 123, and North British Railway 4-4-0 NO. 256 GLEN DOUGLAS, pass Glenoglehead crossing with a Stephenson Locomotive Society special train returning from Oban to Glasgow (Buchanan Street) before descending through Glen Ogle to Lochearnhead. Queen Victoria described this glen as the 'Khyber Pass of Scotland'! For three years this station was the temporary terminus of the line from Dunblane and the original station for the village of Killin. PHOTO: W. A. C. SMITH

21ST AUGUST 1954: A classic view of Callander station from the east. Fairburn Class '4' 2-6-4T No. 42199 awaits departure with the 5.45pm local train to Stirling. A car park now occupies this site. PHOTO: W. A. C. SMITH

30TH MARCH 1959: A busy 'Easter Monday' scene at Callander station. The diesel 'Six Lochs Land Cruise' from Glasgow (Buchanan Street), eventually ending up at Queen Street, stands at the main arrival platform. Next to it is Stanier 4-6-0 No. 45153 heading the 9.18am from Oban to Glasgow (Buchanan Street). Note the Pullman coach behind the engine. 'Black Five' 4-6-0 No. 45213 is on an Up freight, while a horse-box van occupies the dock platform. PHOTO: W. A. C. SMITH

11TH SEPTEMBER 1965: Situated between Callander and Doune was the Drumvaich crossing loop, and Stanier 4-6-0 No. 45359 passes with the 1.18pm from Callander to Glasgow (Buchanan Street). PHOTO: W. A. C. SMITH

10TH OCTOBER 1964: Preserved Caledonian Railway 4-2-2 NO. 123, paired with two restored 'Caley' coaches, is cleared to leave Doune for Callander on the outward journey of a Stephenson Locomotive Society railtour from Glasgow (Buchanan Street). Departing from Glasgow at 13.30 the route was as follows; Stepps – Gartcosh Junction – Garnqueen North Junction – Greenhill Lower Junction - Larbert Junction – Stirling – Dunblane – Doune – arriving at Callander at 14.53. PHOTO: W. A. C. SMITH

THE LMS BEYER-GARRATT 2-6-0+0-6-2

As Britain's economy grew rapidly in the Victorian and early Edwardian era the need to transport raw materials and finished goods in bulk to all parts of the country meant the railways were relied upon to provide this service. In the case of the Midland Railway one of the reasons it existed was to transport vast quantities of coal from the mines of Nottinghamshire and Derbyshire south to the capital leading to a heavy flow of coal traffic on a daily basis.

After Grouping, the LMS initially continued the Midland Railway's 'small engine policy' of hauling trains often using two locomotives of moderate power coupled together. This led to most of the Toton (Nottinghamshire) – Brent (London) coal trains being double-headed by 0-6-0 locomotives, a practice that was understandably uneconomical.

The LMS sought to address this problem by introducing a Garratt locomotive, designed by Fowler, and initially three were ordered from Beyer, Peacock and Company of Gorton, Manchester, with a remit that they would be able to haul around 1,500 tons at 25 mph. However, the LMS Derby design office insisted on, amongst other changes, the fitting of their standard axleboxes to the design. These axleboxes were barely adequate for the LMS Fowler Class 3835 0-6-0 (later referred to as 4F) locomotives, on which they frequently overheated, and as the Garratts were much larger, they unsurprisingly became a major weakness, they were also built with an out-of-date valve gear arrangement and were heavy on coal and maintenance.

The first three locomotives (Nos. 4997-4999) were built in April 1927 and were fitted with vacuum brakes, the remaining 30 (Nos. 4967-4996) were built in the period from August to November 1930. All were built with straight sided bunkers but from 1931 all except the first two of the 1927 trio were fitted with revolving coal bunkers. These were conical in shape and were revolved and oscillated by means of a small 2-cylinder steam engine. The revolving bunkers reduced coal dust from entering the cab and the oscillation facility made them self-trimming, but it was reported that they were still unpopular to drive bunker-first due to dust, and that covers were unsuccessful.

In 1938 the class was renumbered, becoming 7967–7999 in order to make way for the new Stanier 'Black Fives'.

The roundhouses at Toton MPD had to have extra length Garratt roads to accommodate them with others allocated to Wellingborough (where 15 locomotives were located in the 1950s) and Hasland near Chesterfield. As new locomotives were introduced by Stanier they began to be used on other duties including Manchester-bound freights which were generally routed along the Hope Valley Line, the Garratts normally came off their trains at the Gowhole freight sidings just south of Chinley. A few would work the Ambergate to Pye Bridge Line using the north curve at Ambergate, but only as far as Rowsley, where the train would be split. This was normal for goods trains because of the danger of couplings breaking on the climb to Peak Forest. In addition, although they had ample tractive effort to climb the gradient, in the days before goods wagon trains had continuous brakes there were problems on the way down into Chinley. On an early attempt, one of the class was inspected at Heaton Mersey and it was found that all of its brake blocks had melted.

All of the class made it into British Railways service but withdrawals commenced in 1955 as more of the Standard 9Fs became available to replace them, with 47985 the first to go in June of that year, the rest of the class followed quickly and by March 1958 the class had disappeared with the withdrawal of 47994 from Hasland shed, meaning that none of them had completed 30 years service.

LMS BEYER-GARRATT - Specifications	
Builder	Beyer-Peacock
Build date	1927 (3), 1930 (30)
Driving wheels	5ft 3in
Bogie wheels	3ft 3½in
Wheelbase	79ft 0in
Length	87ft 10½in
Loco weight	148 tons 15 cwt (fixed bunker) 155 tons 10 cwt (rotating bunker)
Boiler	Parallel, superheated
Boiler pressure	190psi
Tractive effort	45,620lbs
Coal capacity	1927 built: 7 tons 1930 built: 9 tons
Water capacity	4,500 gallons
Cylinders	Four - 18½in x 26in
Valve gear	Walschaerts

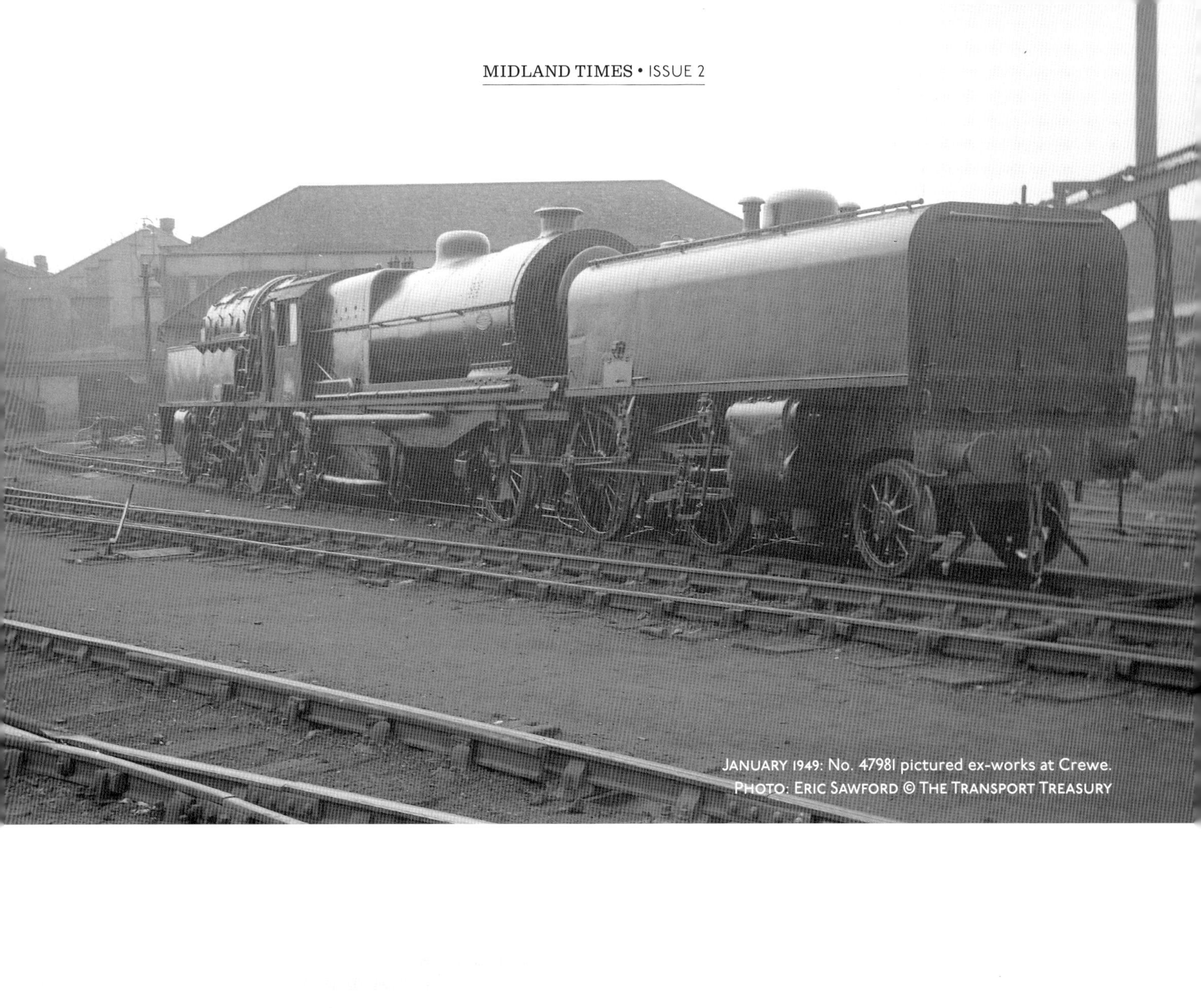

JANUARY 1949: No. 47981 pictured ex-works at Crewe.
PHOTO: ERIC SAWFORD © THE TRANSPORT TREASURY

No. 47988 pictured at Cricklewood, date unknown.
PHOTO: ALEC SWAIN © THE TRANSPORT TREASURY

5TH JUNE 1951: No. 47990 simmers on Wellingborough shed.
PHOTO: ERIC SAWFORD © THE TRANSPORT TREASURY

13TH OCTOBER 1956: No. 47973 on a southbound freight passing through Church Fenton.
PHOTO: MIKE MITCHELL © THE TRANSPORT TREASURY

19TH MARCH 1955: No. 47969 pictured on an Up freight working near Hendon.
PHOTO: R. C. RILEY © THE TRANSPORT TREASURY

1948: No. 47975 retaining LMS lettering on its cabside at Cricklewood shed alongside yet to be renumbered Stanier 8F No. 8334.
PHOTO: JIM HARBERT © THE TRANSPORT TREASURY

4TH APRIL 1954: No. 47991 at Toton shed.
PHOTO: ERIC SAWFORD © THE TRANSPORT TREASURY

THE IRISH MAIL

The Irish Mail operated from London Euston via the West Coast Main Line and North Wales Coast lines to Holyhead, connecting with ferry services to Dublin. The service was introduced by the London & North Western Railway in 1848 but it wasn't until 1927 that it became officially known as 'The Irish Mail' when given the title by the L.M.S.R.

On an unknown date in the 1950s rebuilt 'Patriot' No. 45512 Bunsen is pictured taking water from the troughs at Aber in North Wales.

Photo: A. W. V. Mace © Transport Treasury

REORGANISATION OF CREWE LOCOMOTIVE WORKS, L.M.S.R.

One large shop equipped with the latest appliances replaces nine older erecting shops

Processing or 'belt' system of building and repairing locomotives introduced

Production and transport methods reorganised-time for a heavy locomotive overhaul reduced to a maximum of 12 working days.

Reproduced from 'The Railway Engineer' – July 1928

Crewe Works façade as seen on 3rd April 1966.
Photo: A. E. Bennett © The Transport Treasury

General Introduction

The maintenance of a large stock of locomotives in an efficient state of repair, with, in addition, the building of new engines on a fairly wide scale, is a task involving many difficult problems, and the prevailing conditions of the railway industry demand that the closest possible investigation be applied to the solution of these problems. It is not alone sufficient that the plant available should be of a modern character and that the methods followed in the various shops suffice to ensure a tolerably satisfactory output in what may be termed a "reasonable" amount of time.

Today conditions are such that a railway company, and particularly a grouped railway system owning large numbers of locomotives, must explore every possible avenue of economy, whilst striving at the same time to increase output and always to maintain, if not actually improve, the standard of locomotive upkeep. In point of fact, any new method or system aiming at the betterment of shop conditions in the productive sense must not only reduce the amount of time and labour necessary to achieve the required output, but must, at the same time, increase, wherever possible, the factor of safety as represented by added stringency of inspection and an equal standard of workmanship in the various operations involved. As those acquainted with large locomotive building and repairing establishments are fully aware, such a problem in its every phase demands the closest scrutiny, and not the least of the difficulties to be met is that of co-ordinating efforts throughout the shops and the distribution of the labour forces to the best advantage. Such outstanding matters as transport of material, progressing of work operations, departmental production methods, time and piecework studies, and other items are inseparably bound up with any far-reaching scheme aiming at the systematisation of works operations throughout a large and largely self-contained plant, and these points – to which might be added many more – must be kept in mind in reviewing what has been done at the Crewe works of the London Midland & Scottish Railway, where during the last three years a complete reorganisation, which might aptly be termed a metamorphosis of the whole system of operations, has been carried out. Even a brief survey of this programme of reorganisation suffices to demonstrate the effectiveness of what has been achieved and to indicate the enormous amount of work and study that has been devoted to the problem.

With the exception of one new main building known as the Erecting Shop South, little has been done in the way of adding to or rebuilding the existing shops, the scheme relying for its effectiveness upon the complete recasting of the methods followed in all departments for the purpose of expediting work at every stage, increasing the output of repaired locomotives, in addition to building new ones, at the same time developing an even more thorough system of inspection during repair, and by these combined means securing longer periods of service from locomotives between heavy repairs, which in turn means greater individual engine mileage and more profitable use made of the locomotive stock in general.

Close acquaintance with all that this means and an investigation of the system adopted at Crewe serve conjointly to impress one with the degree of thought and ingenuity with which all the difficulties necessarily arising from such a complete reorganisation have been disposed of. The method adopted of erecting new and repaired locomotives is that known as the processing, or 'Belt' system, one which has hitherto been associated more particularly with automobile construction, the main principle being that every movement and every task associated with the work shall progress in strict accordance with a pre-concerted plan, everything that might be even partly haphazard being rigorously exorcised, and wastage of all kinds ruthlessly cut out. All movements of material and parts are co-ordinated and provided for in a special system of transportation, a time schedule provided for each important movement, and a rule enforced that work once taken up shall not be put down until completed. In the description of the system which follows we shall endeavour to elaborate these points by actual instances of what occurs at various stages of production in the Crewe works, commencing with a general survey of the 'Belt' system, and proceeding thereafter in further articles to individual studies of the methods employed in the numerous departments responsible for the production of new and repaired units, all combining to ensure the objects aimed at as enumerated above.

By the courtesy of Mr. R. W. Reid, C.B.E., Vice-President for Works and Ancillary Undertakings, and of Sir Henry Fowler, K.B.K, Chief Mechanical Engineer, London Midland & Scottish Railway, we were enabled recently to spend some time in the works at Crewe investigating the new system, every assistance and facility being placed at our disposal by Mr. H. P. M. Beames, Mechanical Engineer, Crewe, and members of his staff.

Webb designed LNWR 'Dreadnought' class 2-2-2 No. 3020 pictured on display inside Crewe Works on 23rd February 1936. PHOTO: GEORGE BARLOW © THE TRANSPORT TREASURY

Factors Governing Reorganisation

In reorganising the Crewe works, particular thought and study were devoted not only to the processing of locomotive building and repair operations but also applying the same principle to the production and repair of individual parts. This system ensures that the locomotives in the erecting shop and the components in the various departments pass forward from stage to stage, where all operations are carried out in the correct sequence, the main underlying principles being: (1) that of moving the work to the men rather than the men to the work, and (2) that work shall be carried out continuously – that is to say, any task taken in hand shall be pushed through to completion without any intermediate delays. The need of reorganising the shops was very fully realised after the war when it became possible to resume, on something like normal lines, the maintenance of locomotives, the general condition of which had naturally fallen below the usual standard due to concentration on war work. In 1921 a commencement was made with the building of a new erecting shop at the west end of the works area, this being a definite part of a scheme of improvement in the building and repairing of heavier classes of engines, the intention being to liberate the older erecting shops, of which altogether there were nine, and adapting them for other operations. Owing to the urgent need of economy felt throughout the country, it became necessary to suspend work on the erection of the new shop, and the scheme then in mind was revised, a definite start being made in March 1925, and carried to completion in the comparatively short time of two years. A main difficulty at Crewe in regard to the expansion of the site and buildings is the narrowness of the limits of the works area, expansion being only possible in a westerly direction. The works boundaries in any other direction are represented by the town of Crewe itself and the railway lines to the east and south.

In planning the new system of working it was decided to concentrate in one extensive and modern shop all operations connected with the erection of new and repaired locomotives and of altering, as found necessary, certain other buildings to meet the fresh conditions. An entirely new range of steel-melting furnaces, housed in a new building having the most up-to-date electrical equipment, was laid down. It being found impossible, as already indicated, to expand the works other than longitudinally, and even then only in a limited sense, a scheme to improve the internal system of working and reorganisation of shop methods was concentrated upon, particular regard being paid to the cutting out of all unnecessary transportation. The then existing erecting shops, nine in number, were spread from one end of the works to the other, and there were also two main machine shops, one in the old works at the east end of the site and the other at the west end, the two being probably some

Webb Class G2A No. 49361 being prepared for its duties outside the Steel Foundry (24 on works layout), on 16th February 1964. It was during this week that the loco was transferred from Crewe South (5B) to Bescot (2F).
PHOTO: TONY COUSINS © THE TRANSPORT TREASURY

LNWR Class 317 0-4-2ST No. 47862 stands outside the Signal and Tin Shop (61 and 65 on works layout) shortly before withdrawal from service in 1956. Also known as Saddle Tank Shunter, Dock Tank or Bissel Tanks the class consisted of 20 square saddle-tanked steam locomotives built by the LNWR at Crewe Works between 1896 and 1901. They had a very short coupled wheelbase, with a trailing Bissel truck to carry weight. All passed to the LMS in 1923, who initially allocated them the numbers 6400-6419 in the passenger tank sequence. Only five had been renumbered before the numbers were changed to 7850-7869 in 1927, thus moving them into the goods and shunting tanks, changing their power classification from 1P to 0F at the same time. Only two, 47862 and 47865, survived to enter British Railways service in 1948; 47865 was withdrawn in November 1953, and 47862 three years later.
PHOTO: © THE TRANSPORT TREASURY

1½ miles or more apart. The nine erecting shops aggregated between them 256 engine pits, but with the new progressive arrangement, incorporating the belt system, there are only 72 pits, from which, however, a much larger output is secured, due to the improved methods followed, by means of which the time spent in a heavy overhaul has been reduced from 30, 40, or even 50 days to a present maximum of 12 working days for the largest engines and eight for small 0-6-0 classes.

The reorganisation of individual shops has, wherever necessary, been very completely carried out, the machinery rearranged and much modern plant laid down; whilst, with a view to concentrating definite classes of operations in the same area, complete sets of plant have been moved from one shop to another, the result being seen in greater economy and expedition in building and repairing operations, redundant transport being eliminated and work efficiency improved all round. An entirely new system of reinforced-concrete tractor paths has been laid down to provide roads from the part shops to the erecting shop or finished work stores, as the case may be. Electric and petrol trucks are utilised for the conveyance of material and parts, other

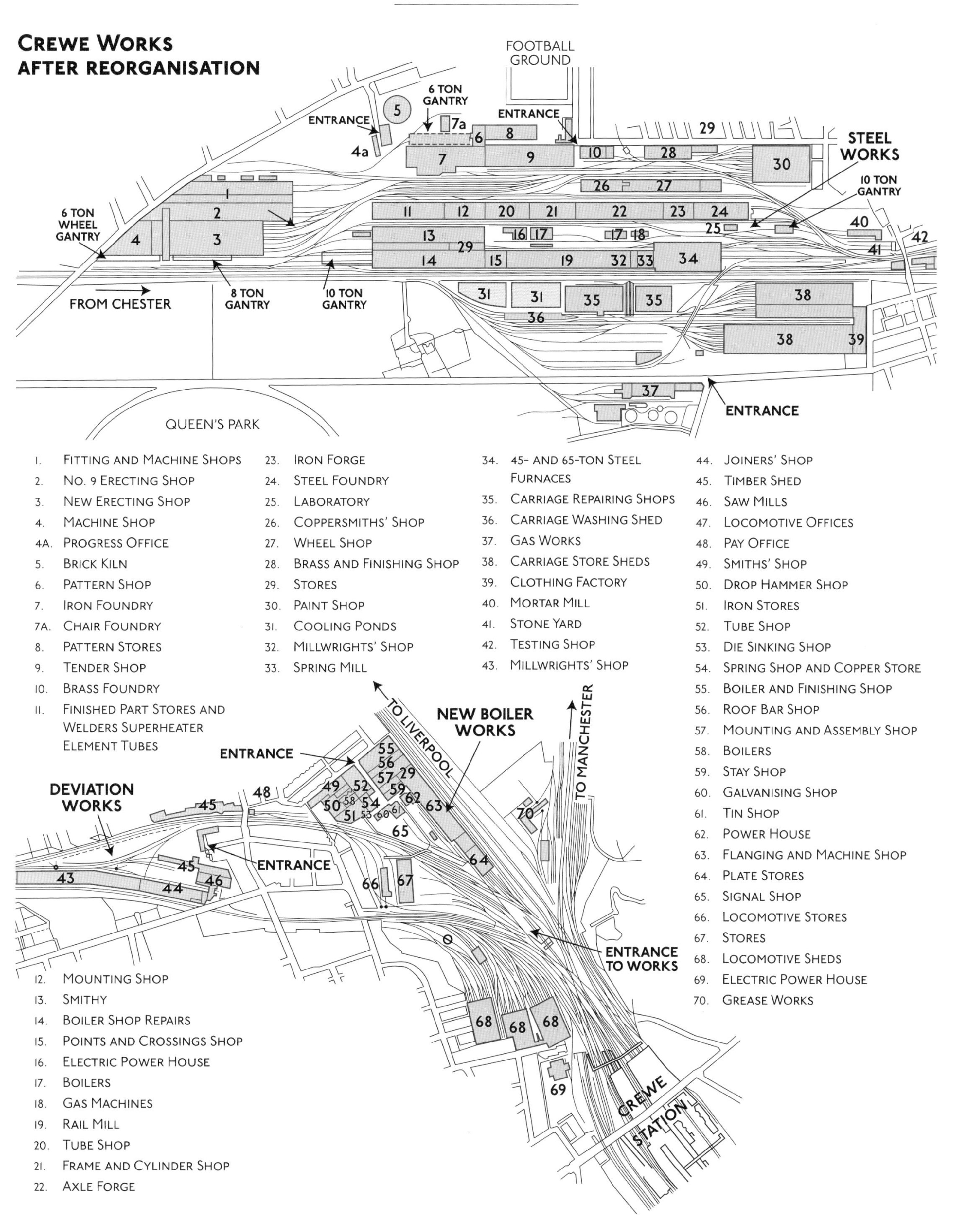
Crewe Works
After Reorganisation
Football Ground
6 Ton Gantry
Entrance
Entrance
Entrance
Steel Works
10 Ton Gantry
6 Ton Wheel Gantry
From Chester
8 Ton Gantry
10 Ton Gantry
Entrance
Queen's Park
To Liverpool
New Boiler Works
To Manchester
Entrance
Deviation Works
Entrance
Entrance to Works
Crewe Station
1. Fitting and Machine Shops
2. No. 9 Erecting Shop
3. New Erecting Shop
4. Machine Shop
4A. Progress Office
5. Brick Kiln
6. Pattern Shop
7. Iron Foundry
7A. Chair Foundry
8. Pattern Stores
9. Tender Shop
10. Brass Foundry
11. Finished Part Stores and Welders Superheater Element Tubes
12. Mounting Shop
13. Smithy
14. Boiler Shop Repairs
15. Points and Crossings Shop
16. Electric Power House
17. Boilers
18. Gas Machines
19. Rail Mill
20. Tube Shop
21. Frame and Cylinder Shop
22. Axle Forge
23. Iron Forge
24. Steel Foundry
25. Laboratory
26. Coppersmiths' Shop
27. Wheel Shop
28. Brass and Finishing Shop
29. Stores
30. Paint Shop
31. Cooling Ponds
32. Millwrights' Shop
33. Spring Mill
34. 45- and 65-ton Steel Furnaces
35. Carriage Repairing Shops
36. Carriage Washing Shed
37. Gas Works
38. Carriage Store Sheds
39. Clothing Factory
40. Mortar Mill
41. Stone Yard
42. Testing Shop
43. Millwrights' Shop
44. Joiners' Shop
45. Timber Shed
46. Saw Mills
47. Locomotive Offices
48. Pay Office
49. Smiths' Shop
50. Drop Hammer Shop
51. Iron Stores
52. Tube Shop
53. Die Sinking Shop
54. Spring Shop and Copper Store
55. Boiler and Finishing Shop
56. Roof Bar Shop
57. Mounting and Assembly Shop
58. Boilers
59. Stay Shop
60. Galvanising Shop
61. Tin Shop
62. Power House
63. Flanging and Machine Shop
64. Plate Stores
65. Signal Shop
66. Locomotive Stores
67. Stores
68. Locomotive Sheds
69. Electric Power House
70. Grease Works

A view from a special train on the Crewe Works branch (the original Chester & Holyhead line) on 3rd April 1966.
PHOTO: A. E. BENNETT © THE TRANSPORT TREASURY

than heavy units, from one section of the works to another. The transportation methods previously employed involved the use of steam shunting locomotives hauling wagons on standard-gauge tracks, a system obviously making for considerable unavoidable delay and lack of economy. The whole of the permanent-way layout in the works area has been remodelled, and now provides accommodation sidings, also facilitating the movement of heavy material such as boilers, etc., taken direct from the erecting to the boiler shop, and vice versa, clear access being provided to any of the bays in the erecting shop, whilst all tracks are interconnected. The locomotives repaired at Crewe belong to the western division of the L.M.S.R., incorporating the whole of the original L. & N.W. and North Staffordshire systems.

THE PROCESSING, OR 'BELT' SYSTEM OF WORKING

Reference was made above to the association between the processing, or belt system of working and the automobile industry, but the application of this principle at Crewe necessarily differs somewhat in detail from that followed in a motor car factory, for the reason that the size and weight of the individual units and their parts are greater and the number of operations increased, whilst movements are naturally slower. The new erecting shop consists of three bays, the greatest length of the building being 910 ft. and the total width 194 ft., the height to the eaves being 35 ft. The building is located at the extreme west end of the works area, parallel with the machine shop and old (No. 9) erecting shop. The new erecting shop is fully equipped with compressed-air appliances, the mains being carried along the floor parallel to the pits and tapped at engine lengths. The whole of the shop is electrically wired for power and lighting, and electrically operated portable cylinder-boring and port-facing machines are employed.

Each of the three bays has two pit roads or belts. Four of the six belts are at present in use, three of them having 12, and the remaining one, eight stages. Each belt provides one completed engine per day, or six per week, whilst in addition, six heavy repairs are completed on the "group" system, these being of irregular types. Under this latter system of repairing engines, the men are employed in groups doing regular work, such as stripping groups, assembling and finishing groups, various stages of the work being undertaken by the particular groups allocated to these specific parts. The stripping groups are stationary, but the assembling and finishing groups pass from engine to engine within certain areas. As the belt system is developed, these types will also be repaired in accordance therewith, and the group system discontinued. An additional centre road, without pits, traverses the length of the bay, this being used for traffic purposes, i.e., conveyance of material, etc. The complete shop provides on the six belts, 72 repair stages in all, but, as previously explained, only four belts are at present employed. Each stage is allocated for specified classes of repair operations. Of the 12 stages, the first two are devoted to the work of stripping an engine, when it is completed, being moved forward to one of the succeeding four stages, where it stands for four days, during which time repairs are carried out to the frames, cylinders, etc. On completion of stripping, one engine frame is placed on its stand on one of the four adjoining positions in the bay, these positions being numbered stages 1, 2, 3 and 4. The work gangs, of which there are four, move between stages 1, 2, 3 and 4 as they finish their own particular tasks at a stage. As explained, four working days are allowed for an engine frame to remain on its stand. On the fifth day the intermediate and bogie wheels have been returned duly repaired, and ready for the frame and boiler from one of the four stages to be lifted on to the wheels.

ENGINE MOVEMENTS AND OUTPUT

The movements so far are effected by means of overhead electric cranes which span the pits in each bay. These cranes, which are of 50 tons capacity, have each four motors, and there are also three 10-ton, 3-motor overhead cranes, with an additional crane in the south bay to deal with wheels. These cranes were manufactured by Sir William Arrol & Co. Ltd. On reaching the fifth stage the engine is lowered on to its intermediate and bogie wheels, and then moves forward to stage 6, at which it becomes one of a series of six engines connected together by a steel cable operated by 10-ton winches at ground level outside the shop, the engines being moved forward from stage to stage by the winches at a definite period during the day, until on the 12th day an engine has reached the final stage, and is pulled out of the shop by the winch as a completed unit. These winches were supplied by S. H. Heywood & Co. Ltd, of Reddish, Stockport. By this means it is possible to keep a certain amount of specified work at definite points in the shop. The result is seen in the liberation from each belt for every day of 7 hours 50 minutes working time of an engine completed and ready for test, having been completely repaired within 12 days from the time it arrived at the first pit. This applies to the largest and heaviest types, whereas for the smaller types the time occupied is reduced to eight days. The capacity of the shop as a whole is 66 engines, taking the engine length, plus an allowance for a gap between each engine, as 42½ ft., and the output from the shop is equal to 30 to 35 heavy repairs per week and 100 new locomotives per annum.

Since the first engine was turned out by this system on 5th May 1927, over 850 locomotives have been repaired without any delay whatsoever. It is possible to have as many as five different classes of engine on an individual belt at one time, this being alone made practicable by the fact that the repairs to all the component parts are processed in the same manner, the processing of the locomotive itself being the final result of the system generally. Stacking grounds are provided for storing wheels, and another for cabs, panels, splashers and other material not immediately requiring repairs. These spaces are provided with overhead gantry cranes, by means of which the transference of the various units and classes of material from point to point is quickly effected. These storing grounds are immediately adjacent to the erecting shops. A feature of the erecting shop is that very few fitters' benches are in evidence, whilst in no case is there cupboard accommodation or tool receptacles provided, tools being contained in portable iron chests mounted on wheels, which enable them to be moved about to the job where the men are engaged. A strong point in connection with the shop is that no material is allowed to lie about, all material and parts being brought, as already stated, to the stages at which they are required two hours before being wanted. This ensures that there shall be no congestion of material that is either not required or will not be required for some time ahead.

The warming of the erecting shop is effected by means of steam, the heating pipes being located overhead. This proves effective as it operates on the principle of warming the upper air first, so that the warmth may descend instead of rising to the upper level and losing some of its value by dissipation, as is so often the case when the heating arrangements are placed at ground level. The system is split up into 12 sets of pipes, each set consisting of one steam-flow pipe and two return pipes. Two sets are located on either side of each erecting shop and machine-shop bay, and are placed above the bottom tie of the roof principal. The condensate is returned to the boiler as feed water. The whole of the system is divided into four main portions for the purpose of providing efficient circulation, main steam supplies being taken at three points. With this system it has been found possible to maintain an inside temperature of 55 degrees Fahrenheit when the temperature outside is at freezing point. Four water-tube boilers are installed, three working and one stand-by. These, in addition to supplying steam for heating the new erecting shop, also provide for the heating of No. 9 Erecting Shop, the machine shop, and all boshes.

It is interesting to record that the use of daylight has been exploited to the full in the design of the new erecting shop at Crewe. The whole of the six slopes are entirely covered with glass, which, in addition to offering the required lighting facilities, acts as a permanent roof covering free from maintenance charges beyond cleaning and replacement of occasional breakages. The glazing contract was entrusted to Mellowes & Co. Ltd, of Sheffield, who executed the work on their 'Eclipse' system of patent glazing. The total area of glazing involved is approximately 181,000 sup. ft.

Timing and Material Schedules

Clocks are placed in conspicuous positions in the shop, showing for each belt the time of the next movement of engines. These, of course, are merely dummy clocks, the indications being made by moving the hands to the required setting. The clocks are painted bright red with white lettering and figures. The illustration below shows clocks in adjoining bays set to indicate that the next moves will occur on Thursday at 11.30 and Friday at 9.15. It is definitely laid down that specified classes of work are to be performed only at each stage, the necessary material and parts being delivered

from the various shops at those stages two hours before the engine is due to arrive at that stage. This rule, strictly enforced, ensures that no delay is caused in going on with the work as soon as the engine reaches any particular stage. Schedules are issued for separate classes of engines, stating what material has to be at each stage in anticipation of requirements, thus giving the shop concerned ample notice in advance. Special appliances to enable work to be carried out quickly and easily are employed. With a system such as this greater use can be made of such appliances, as they are needed at only one point in the erecting shop and there is no necessity, therefore, to spend time in looking for a tool or appliance, or, indeed, for anything required for the execution of the task. Platforms provided with wheels are used to enable the men to reach the tops of the boilers and other elevated positions, these platforms being readily moved from point to point or from engine to engine as required. In addition, there are numerous other special appliances designed to facilitate work of various kinds and reduce the amount of time and labour involved. Some of these, notably a wheeled trolley for placing ashpans in position, raising appliances for vacuum cylinders and so forth, the purpose being to reduce to a minimum manhandling of material and parts.

The location of the engines at their different stages on a belt, from the first, or stripping stage, to the last, or completion stage are reproduced in a simplified form herewith and in correct sequence. These, of course, are additional to the stripping operations which occur prior to reaching stage 1.

STAGE 1. Cleaning tops of cylinders, ends and covers; examination of frames and cylinders. Removing steam-chest liners; drilling studs, set-screws, etc., on cylinders and frames, and welding any cracks. Welding frames; replacing drag box; (boring cylinder); fitting studs.

STAGE 2. (Fitting steam-chest liners); refitting pivot casting; (chipping and grinding frames after welding). Boring steam-chest liners; replacing hornblock patches. Remaking back cylinder cover joints.

STAGE 3. Setting slide-bars; fitting hornblock keeps; straightening front end. Setting radius-rod brackets; fitting studs for guide brackets; filing hornblocks. Mounting boiler in frame and bolting up.

STAGE 4. Fitting 3½ in. exhaust-pipe brackets, wash-out plugs, and blow-off cock; mounting whistle stand. Mounting cylinder cocks and gear, intermediate oil pipes, safety-valve and fitting crossheads. Fitting pistons and rings, cylinder covers and packing. Lagging ashpan and fitting damper doors.

STAGE 5. Adding radial truck and intermediate wheels under engine. Mounting vacuum sack and brackets, buffer plank, draw bar hook, increased brake guide or rocking-shaft brackets, piston valves, damper gear and part of lubricator gear.

Thereafter the locomotive is hauled down the shop to stages 6, 7, 8, 9 and 10, moving one stage per day. Each day the following work is carried out:

STAGE 6. Mounting buffers, stiffening plates, lamp brackets, snifting valves, and air pump. Fitting panels, expansion brackets, dirt plates, reversing screw and rods, reversing-shaft quadrants, etc., and rocking gear.

STAGE 7. Carrying out part of smokebox work, mounting steam pipes and bolting up smokebox. Mounting injector and cab, locking gear, sand gear and lubrication to axleboxes. Refitting splashers, sand boxes and footsteps.

STAGE 8. Completing smokebox work; finishing cab and footplate; fitting 3½ in. exhaust pipe. Mounting mechanical or Detroit lubricator and pumping oil through.

STAGE 9. Mounting wheels and setting in position. Fitting up motion and connecting rods. Wheeling engines, bolting up hornblock keeps, stays, centre-bearing wedges and cap. Fitting radial truck pivot studs and nuts, cylinder-cock pipes and brackets, oil pipes and brackets.

STAGE 10. Fitting up brakework, coupling rods, crank-pin washers, sand pipes and stays. Assisting valve setters. Fitting steam-chest covers, covering plates and door. Adjusting weight and lifting engine off pit.

How Engines enter and leave the Shop

The engines are brought into the erecting shop from outside by means of an electrically-operated traverser fitted with electric wind for hauling locomotives on or off the tracks. This traverser runs the whole width of the shop and also that of the old (No. 9) erecting shop, or erecting shop north, as it is marked on the plan, the total traverse being 300 feet. Reference has already been made to the fact that electrically operated winches are employed for actuating the steel wire cables which draw the engines along the belt. The two winches are suitably housed to protect them from the weather, and each operates cables for three belts and centre roads, the cables running around bollards which guide them and allow them to exert a direct pull in alignment with the string of engines moving along an individual belt.

It has thus been briefly shown how the belt system of locomotive repair operates in principle, but it may be added that the men engaged at each stage along the belt are expert in the

Fowler 4F Class 0-6-0 Nos. 4563 and 4564 under construction at Crewe Works in 1937. PHOTO: A. W. V. MACE © THE TRANSPORT TREASURY

particular tasks to be performed. Having had the opportunity of observing the work in progress in the erecting shop, we are able to state from personal observation that everything appears to work with the utmost smoothness and regularity, the time-keeping being throughout of the most accurate description. Before the winches are put into operation to effect the movement of a locomotive along the belt in accordance with the clock indications, a loud buzzer is sounded to give the signal, the various gangs of workmen then being made aware of the fact that the movement is about to take place. A locomotive after leaving the shop has its tender attached and is then steamed, afterwards going for a trial trip. It is then either taken to the paint shop or retained by the Motive Power Department for service.

The Progress Office – a controlling factor

Having thus briefly outlined the main principle involved, in so far as the physical factors are concerned, it will be of interest to devote attention to the control of the system and the manner in which correct inter-departmental functioning is assured. If such a system as this is to be successful it must necessarily rely basically upon a clear understanding between those in charge of the numerous departments concerned, and this, as a matter of course, applies to all grades, i.e., the managerial staff, foremen, leading hands, and, indeed, everyone concerned with the task in hand. Careful records must be kept of what is being done, and daily programmes of work arranged for. The whole of these important functions are vested in a special department known as the Progress Office, those in charge being responsible under the Mechanical Engineer and Works Manager for planning all the numerous operations and seeing that they are carried out strictly in conformity with the system laid down. Thus the whole of the operations heretofore referred to are based upon a definite system of work processing. The Progress Office controls the shopping of the engines, inspection, manufacture of the parts required and the repairs to be carried out, careful records being kept of every phase of the work. A short meeting takes place daily in the Progress Office, this being attended by certain foremen under the chairmanship of a Progress Department assistant. At these meetings the agenda covers the supply of all material and the conveyance of the Works Manager's instructions to the various shops. Any difficulties arising in connection with the supply of parts are discussed and measures taken to overcome them. This ensures a free and open discussion among the foremen of the shops concerned, so that any matter arising can be thrashed out on the spot and disposed of. The minutes of the meetings are published daily, each shop in the works receiving a copy. Certain out-station sheds attached to the Particulars of Work Chief Mechanical Engineer's Department also receive copies of these

Webb 'Coal Tank' No. 27645 in Crewe Works ready to receive attention on 3rd March 1935.
PHOTO: GEORGE BARLOW © THE TRANSPORT TREASURY

minutes, which daily show the number of engines to be taken in for the various belts on the following day. Upon receipt of these engine numbers, the machine and other part shops at once notify the various leading hands as to the dates on which the particular materials for which they are responsible will be required. This information is entered up on a progress sheet supplied to each leading hand, and from which the foremen of the shops can ascertain whether a particular job is behindhand or not.

The Shopping of Engines

The starting point at which the scheme comes into operation is that of keeping track of the condition of all locomotives belonging to the division in service. The length of time from the last heavy repair until the engine is considered for the next overhaul is fixed-for the larger passenger engines at 12 months, and for freight engines at from 18 to as much as 30 months – and a sheet is issued under the heading of "Shopping of Engines", on which is set forth the various classes of engines and the periods allocated as the minimum bases for heavy overhaul periods. It is not, however, drastically laid down that at the end of that time the engines must necessarily come into the shop for repair on the belts. Special forms are issued to the running sheds, and on these the condition of a given engine must be entered up two months before it is due, not definitely for actual shopping, but for the "proposal for shopping", which, in other words, means that at ten months from the time a passenger engine left the shops either as new or after heavy repairs, a careful investigation must be carried out as to its condition and a report made to enable the progress office to decide whether or not, according to the information given, the engine can be relied upon to continue in service after the prescribed period. Two forms are sent out, one relating to the frames, cylinders, wheels and motion, and the other to the boiler. The forms when completed are sent to the mechanical engineer, and from these reports the engine referred to is definitely scheduled for shopping, or alternatively, allowed to continue in service for a further period. Two months prior to the conclusion of the further period the same procedure is repeated, and at the expiration of that time, or even later, it is often found that the locomotive is still fit to continue working. This arrangement not only ensures that the last available mile is got out of the engine, but also makes certain of a thorough and systematic periodical inspection. It is of interest to note that 10,000 locomotives on the L.M.S. Railway are being regularly watched in this manner.

The Recording System

Paramount filing cards are utilised for recording the T proposals and re-proposals of engines for repairs, one of these cards being reproduced below. It relates to an 'Experiment' 4-6-0 type passenger locomotive numbered 887 under the old classification, and 5496 under the new or grouped classification. The card indicates that the engine is located at shed No. 19, the date of the initial proposal for shopping being shown and also the subsequent dates entered up after the shopping reports have been considered, whilst finally the date decided upon for actual shopping, due to the condition of the engine, is indicated. The numbers on the left-hand side and top of the card indicate the various classes of engines, whilst the entries on the right-hand side show the general class of engine and particulars of heavy renewals required, i.e., cylinders, boiler or tyres. The card is gang punched where necessary. The card reproduced shows that the engine belongs to class 6A and that it requires heavy repairs to cylinders, boilers and tyres, this being perhaps an extreme case. It will be further

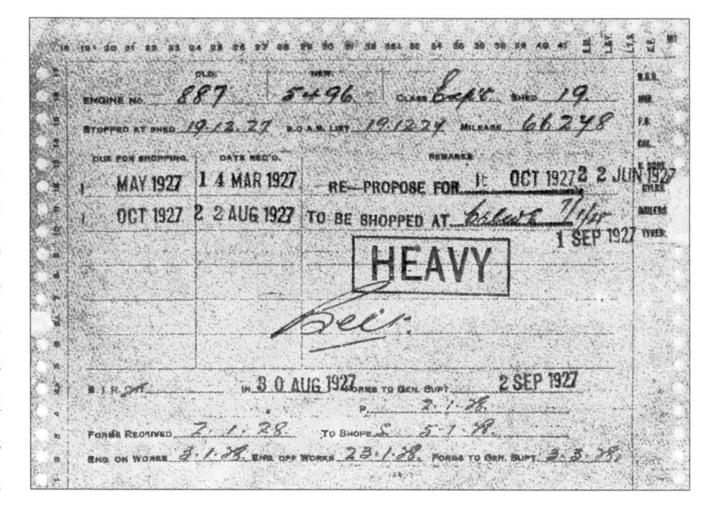
ENGINE NO. OLD 887 NEW 5496 CLASS Expt. SHED 19.
STOPPED AT SHED 19.12.27 MILEAGE 66278

DUE FOR SHOPPING.	DATE REC'D.	REMARKS
MAY 1927	14 MAR 1927	RE-PROPOSE FOR OCT 1927 22 JUN 1927
OCT 1927	22 AUG 1927	TO BE SHOPPED AT 1 SEP 1927

HEAVY

IN 30 AUG 1927 FORMS TO GEN. SUPT. 2 SEP 1927
P. 7.1.28.
FORMS RECEIVED 7.1.28. TO SHOPS 5.1.28.
ENG. ON WORKS 3.1.28. ENG. OFF WORKS 23.1.28. FORMS TO GEN. SUPT. 3.3.28.

noticed that the engine completed no less a mileage than 66,278 since the last heavy shopping, and it has been 're-proposed' twice, the result being that although due for shopping in May 1927, it remained in service until 3rd January 1928, being returned to service after test runs on the 23rd of the same month. On the decision being reached to shop an engine, notification is sent to the General Superintendent, Derby, through the Motive Power Department, of the withdrawal of the engine from service, and the General Superintendent is again notified through the same channels when the repairs have been completed and the engine is again available for work. It will be noticed that the paramount card shows the dates on which these notifications were sent in each case. Each week a summary is made of those engines agreed for shopping and typed copies of this summary are sent to the various shop foremen, who then know what engines are coming along, also whether new parts are required, such as tyres, cylinders, motion details, etc. Weekly lists of the engine requirements necessary to keep the belts active are sent to the Motive Power Superintendent, these relating to requirements for the following week, and he selects from those engines already agreed for shopping by the Mechanical Engineer's Department, the selection being based on the classes of engines which can best be spared in accordance with the exigencies of traffic at the time. This list covers the number of engines required each day to feed the erecting shop.

Sequence of Operations

Summarised, the sequence of events is as follows:

1. Two months before the expiry of the 12-month period (for passenger locomotives), the Motive Power Department, after an examination, sends a report to the Mechanical Engineer's Department as to the condition of the engine.
2. The Mechanical Engineer sends out a Boiler Inspector to examine the boiler and make a report as to the condition of the same and what will be its probable life without further repairs.
3. The Mechanical Engineer's Department then examines both the Motive Power Department report and their Boiler Inspector's report, and either accepts the engine or re-proposes it for a further period.
4. The list is circulated throughout the works departments so that every individual shop foreman is aware of what engines are coming in, and by reference to the previous list – supplied when engines were agreed for shopping – the foreman can ascertain what heavy parts are required.
5. Steps are then taken to see that the necessary cylinders, tyres, etc., are ready for the engines as required.

Engines from the various running sheds are worked to the Crewe sheds and brought into the works strictly in accordance with scheduled arrangements. On arrival in the works yard, the tender, where such is fitted, is taken off the engine and sent to the tender shop, where the heaviest repairs possible to a tender must not exceed four days. This means that the tender can, at the end of that period, be returned to traffic, that is, several days before the locomotive itself is ready. It has been the policy at Crewe for long past to have fewer tenders than engines, thus not only avoiding loss of mileage and consequent revenue, but also avoiding congestion of the yards, and the loss represented by a considerable amount of demobilised capital. Locomotive tenders are repaired, as in the case of the engines themselves, on the belt system. If any delay should take place in the supply of the material to the belt, this is immediately reported on small slips, one copy being sent to the Works Manager direct, and another copy to the Progress Office, where the point raised is dealt with at once, the office finally reporting the whole of the circumstances to the Works Manager, who connects this report up with the slip previously sent direct to him by the erecting shop, the matter then being taken up with the person primarily concerned.

Rigid Inspection Methods

In order to ensure that each engine is given a thorough and complete repair, a rigid system of inspection has been put in force making possible rapid decisions as to the actual repairs to be undertaken; also ensuring that no part whatsoever goes into service in a defective condition. In accordance with this system of inspection, special men are engaged solely in examining boilers, cylinders, motion details, frames, axles, wheels, etc., each being a specialist in his own sphere. The inspectors are supplied with forms on which they enter details of the work required on the particular items. These are sent to the foremen of the various shops and the job cards for the men are made out and checked, these cards being compiled from the inspectors' forms by men working under the foremen, thus ensuring that only such work as is really necessary is actually done on the locomotive parts. The results of the inspector's examination of various parts are entered up as a continuous record, the entries being made by the inspector who examines the part, and signed by him, so that the responsibility for the examination is definitely fixed. Similarly, any particular repair carried out at the previous overhaul can be followed up and whether such repair proved to be thorough or expedient ascertained. From these records much valuable information is obtained as to the advisability of repairing, or, alternatively, renewing various items of construction.

Webb 0-4-2WT Crane Tank No. 3249 in ex-shops condition at Crewe on 20th August 1939.
PHOTO: GEORGE BARLOW © THE TRANSPORT TREASURY

Webb Class 2F 0-6-0 Coal Engine No. 58328 hauls a freight through Crewe Works Yard on 12th August 1952.
PHOTO: ERIC SAWFORD © THE TRANSPORT TREASURY

Built for the Caledonian Railway at St. Rollox Works, Glasgow in 1895, Class 264 0-4-0ST No. 56027 is seen working as the Crewe Works pilot. It was transferred to Crewe from Preston in January 1957 and worked there until withdrawal from service in October 1960. Note the coal stored on the cab roof.
PHOTO: ALEC SWAIN © THE TRANSPORT TREASURY

The inspectors' reports, or as they are termed, "Inspection and Repair Notes", cover the whole range of the locomotive and its parts, separate forms being entered up under the headings of Welding – Frames – Wheels, Driving, Intermediate and Trailing – Spring Gear – Connecting Rods – Coupling Rods – Slide Bars – Motion Details – Reversing Gear – Piston and Valves – Cylinders – Brake Work, and Tender Details. It is possible to obtain without any difficulty from these various inspection and repair notes or forms a knowledge of the parts to be renewed or repaired, the information being classified under the headings – Item – No. to be Renewed – No. to be Repaired – Remarks – Amount of Piecework Prices. The number of the engine and its class are given, and on some of the forms the number of the belt on which the work is to be done. The forms used for the wheels provide for entries relating to journals, crank pins, etc.

A similar series of forms is used for recording the actual work done on the engines covering the whole of the range indicated above on the inspectors' forms. Some of the latter series are accompanied by sketches graphically indicating repairs, and as an example the set before us at the time of writing contains sketches of main frames on which some minor welding operations have been carried out, the location of these being ascertainable at a glance and their character briefly set out on the drawing. These reports are signed by the persons responsible and give the date on which the work was done, the number of the engine, the shop, the original date of construction, and the foremen's signatures.

Limits of wear are strictly laid down and are worked to by means of limit gauges by the inspectors, so that a uniform standard of repair is maintained. The limit system is based on the "Unilateral" principle, with the hole as a base, plus allowance on the standard and minus allowance on the shaft. A standardised supply of limit gauges is available.

A very complete range of standard graduated sizes of motion pins, valves, etc., is in operation at Crewe. All motion pins are machined in graduations of 0.005 in. between sizes, so that the largest diameter of pin when worn is merely ground to the next size below and becomes available for further use in another engine. The whole of the inspection and the issuing of the necessary instructions for repairs is carried out within the first two days of the engine being taken into the shop. Simultaneously with the stripping-down operation, parts taken off the engine are placed in pans or containers alongside the engine. These pans are placed in the bosh cleaning plant, after which the parts are inspected and sent to the various repair shops for repair or renewal as the case may be, being returned, as already stated, to

The machine shop area at the west end of the new Erecting Shop (3 on works layout).

the belt stage at which they will be mounted on the engine two hours before they are required.

The method followed by the inspectors is an extremely thorough one. All rods and motion parts are examined minutely for flaws by tapping the rod or part with a light hammer, the purpose being to set up vibration, which causes oil to exude from any fracture which may exist. The parts having been taken off engines newly arrived from service, naturally carry a film of oil, and after the first tapping, the part affected is wiped dry and again tapped, when even a minute or hair crack will be at once discovered by further oil showing on the surface. All rods containing flaws are replaced by new ones, and although the method is such an apparently simple one, it is found to be entirely effective – indeed, it is rarely if ever that even a small defect escapes notice. Wheels undergoing inspection are allowed to fall from a height of about 10 inches on to a track in the shop. They are pushed along a rail bearing platform, and the jolt from the higher to the lower level sets up vibrations throughout the whole of the wheels, thus producing the same effect as the hammering just described, in that it brings out any oil to indicate the location of a fracture. The whole of the journals and crank pins are examined for flaws and measured over for wear. If fit to run again, the size of the journal and pin is taken by micrometer, and the sizes handed to the machine shop foreman, so that the rods and axleboxes can be bored to suit. The whole of this inspection is, as previously stated, completed during the initial period of two days, namely, while the engine is at the stripping positions. So thorough, indeed, is the inspection, that rod examination alone represents a continuous process, and when it is remembered that rods belonging to as many as 30 to 33 engines are examined every week, some idea of the magnitude of the task can be gathered. A certain amount of machining work is carried out in the erecting shop, where a machine section is installed, this including tyre turning, journal skimming, and work on axleboxes, coupling and connecting rods. In the axlebox department, the principle in force is that axleboxes once picked up off the ground are not put down until completed, passing from machine to machine on a runway, the machines being so arranged that the operations follow in correct sequence, all being at the same level.

Locomotive cabs, bunkers, tanks and panels are built and repaired on the belt system, being moved on trolleys at definite periods and passing from gang to gang at stated times, the work being so co-ordinated that each particular item is repaired, and, in the case of tanks, tested in sufficient time to be at its allotted stage in the correct order. The belts for tanks, cabs, etc., are located in the old erecting shop, No. 9, now referred to as Erecting Shop North, which lies parallel to the new shop, and the parts stripped from the engine are conveyed by the traverser to the old erecting shop. They are there examined and repaired and passed along parallel with the pits in the new erecting shop, and again enter the shop on the centre road where they meet the engine to which they belong and are mounted in position. These parts are transferred from the belt to the centre bay of the erecting shop by means of bogies moving along a path which extends the whole width of the old and present erecting shops, and the old machine shop at the east end of the building.

The repair of locomotive tenders is carried out in a separate building, again on the belt system. Two belts, each consisting of eight tenders, are in operation, the tenders being brought in on the traverser and taken out in the same manner. A move along the belt takes place every four hours, and 11 repaired tenders of all classes are obtained each week off each belt, this number being sufficient to meet normal requirements.

Progress Boards and Forms

Among the forms used in connection with the progress system is one showing the position of engines under and awaiting repairs. This is supplied to the Works Manager from the Progress Office and reviewed by him weekly. The Progress Office makes up a return from special boards, on which are shown the daily movements of the locomotives, so that no engine can possibly be lost sight of. Discs are hung on these boards, each disc bearing the number of the engine which comes under the Chief Mechanical Engineer's department, various columns being provided with headings such as 'Stopped at Sheds', 'Awaiting Repairs in Yard', or 'In Shops under Repair'. The discs progress with the movements of the engines themselves, and it can therefore be seen almost at a glance exactly where a particular engine is at the moment.

A boiler progress board is also employed in the office for showing the position of the stock of spare boilers, i.e., whether awaiting or under repairs, being mounted on frames or placed on the reserve stock, and this ensures that the location of every boiler can be readily seen and such boilers as may be required in the immediate future given preference. On this board, progress tickets take the place of the discs, and these tickets are changed daily in accordance with the actual state of the boiler concerned. The entries on the tickets give the number of the boiler, the number of the engine from which it came, when the repair began, when completed and so on, and a summary made from these boards is sent to the Works Manager each week.

What the System has Achieved

The results obtained from the 'reorganisation' of Crewe Works as described above were summarised by Mr. Beames in his paper on the subject before the Institution of Mechanical Engineers, as follows:

1. Reduction of transport costs.
2. Decreased manufacturing costs of steel, locomotives, boilers, and all components.
3. Increased output of repairs and renewals, with decrease in overtime and night-shift working.
4. Decrease in time locomotives out of traffic, and consequently, lower stock of locomotives required.
5. Reduction in quantity of portable tools and in labour costs
6. Lower supervision costs in erecting shop.
7. Decreased cost of electric current and of gas.
8. Greater ability to cope with the increased size of locomotives and the extra requirements due to the grouping of the railways.

In addition, it may be remarked that the adoption of the system has reduced very considerably the number of engines engaged in shunting operations within the works area, the actual figure being at least 20 per cent, whilst the number of wagons employed for conveying material has been reduced by 60 per cent. There has, further, been a reduction in the number of men employed – not, however, by discharges, but due to the fact that the necessity of replacing those who have retired or for any other reason have left the company's employment has disappeared, it having been anticipated all along that with the development of the system less labour would be required.

It is an outstanding factor that, whilst the scheme undoubtedly benefits the railway company, the men themselves earn higher wages, and it was, and is, the company's desire that the men should share in the advantages gained. Further economy is represented by the fact that the work flows all in one direction – namely, from east to west – raw materials, etc., entering at the east end and progressing through the various departments until reaching the point at which they are required for assembly on the engines on the west end, the idea being to ensure that there is no turning back at any point. The complete engines traverse the works area from west to east, passing out into service in the yards at that end. It might be inferred that a system of this kind, whilst greatly facilitating operations in the erecting shop; would, owing to the time limit placed on every stage of production, lead to greater hustle in the machine and other part shops – or, in other words, whilst the erectors have an easier time, the fitters and machinists have to work at higher pressure. This, however, is not the case, one explanation being that a job once taken up is pushed through to a finish without being allowed to stand down for indefinite periods, as was previously the case. Another point to be remembered is that in the machine and fitting shops, the individual parts of engines are dealt with, as in the erecting shop are the locomotives themselves, on the processing, or belt system. It is a case of quicker and better organised, rather than more work, advantage being gained by the subdivision of labour, so that what might have taken one man a fortnight to complete is now put through by four men in a fraction of the time.

THE PLATFORM END

Picture: Edinburgh Princes Street on 12th February 1965.

In future issues our aim is to bring you many differing articles about the LMS, its constituent companies and the London Midland Region of British Railways. We hope to have gone some way to achieving this in Issue 2.

Midland Times welcomes constructive comment from readers either by way of additional information on subjects already published or suggestions for new topics that you would like to see addressed. The size and diversity of the LMS, due to it being comprised of many different companies each with their differing ways of operating, shows the complexity of the subject and we will endeavour to be as accurate as possible but would appreciate any comments to the contrary.

We want to use these final pages as your platform for comment and discussion so please feel free to send your comments to:
midlandtimes1884@gmail.com or write to:
Midland Times, Transport Treasury Publishing Ltd., 16 Highworth Close, High Wycombe HP13 7PJ.

THE PLATFORM END - READER'S LETTERS

Dear Mr. Sikes

Midland Times' appearance is the best thing since Midland Record and LMS Journal, well done! You mention in 'Platform End' in the first edition that you welcome constructive comments so I hope that this is of interest.

In the item on the LMS's constituents, you note that the 'County Donegal Railway Joint Committee Lines' were "Operated jointly by the NCC and Great Northern of Ireland (GNR(I)) these became joint lines of the LMS and GNR(I) after grouping". This is actually the latest in a whole series of ever so slightly incorrect statements about the ownership of or responsibility for the CDJR. For anyone interested in corporate history particularly that of the Midland, it is a fascinating and very complex tale.

The Donegal Railway was a company incorporated by Act of Parliament, which was a combination of the Finn Valley Railway and the West Donegal Railway company. The Finn Valley was built to the Irish Standard Gauge whilst the West Donegal was 3ft gauge. Oddly, the FVR was worked by the GNR(I) whilst the West Donegal was worked by the FVR, using locomotives and rolling stock owned by the WDR. The West Donegal aiming to link Stranorlar and Donegal, ran out of cash at a place called Druminin, where it built a temporary station. A light railway order (not under the Light Railway Act of 1896 which was a decade in the future, but issued by the Board of Trade) permitted the building of the West Donegal Light Railway (which legally was part of the WDR, not a separate company) to link Druminin with Donegal. However, there was not enough money to build a station at Donegal, so another company, the Donegal Railway Station Company was created to build the station there and rent it to the WDR for £200 per year from opening of the station and light railway in 1888.

Following a Royal Commission, there was then a series of 3ft gauge lines built that linked to the Stranorlar to Donegal route. Privately promoted but with a government guarantee, these were the West Donegal Light Railway (Donegal to Killybegs) and the Finn Valley (Stranorlar & Glenties) Railway. These were both 3ft gauge; this entire 3ft gauge system led to Stranorlar, where the Finn Valley line provided the trunk of the system, taking it on the 5ft 3in gauge to Strabane, where it met the Great Northern Railway of Ireland. In 1892, all these narrow gauge companies, and the FVR amalgamated to form the Donegal Railway Company which changed the gauge of the FVR to 3ft thus making the entire system 3ft gauge.

None of this considerable network was particularly profitable, yet two extensions were promoted. They were accounted for separately, but formed a legal part of the DR. One was from Strabane to Londonderry and the other from Donegal to Ballyshannon. The Donegal Railway Act of 7th August 1896 allowed their building and the raising by the DR of £100,000 in ordinary shares, £40,000 in 4% preference shares and £70,000 in 4% debentures, apparently without any difficulty. How a company which a few years before could not afford to build its terminal station could hope to raise this, or in fact did raise this, is a matter of speculation. Perhaps significantly, the Londonderry line was built first and opened on 1st August 1900.

The Midland Railway's Heysham Harbour Act had been obtained in 1892 and work began building the harbour and railway in 1898. The MR was always on the look out for opportunities for profitable expansion, which usually meant extending the system, or at least its operations by running powers, to the ultimate source of its traffic; its line to Swansea is a classic of this mindset. In the case of Ireland, the Belfast and Northern Counties Railway (BNCR) had its main line from Belfast to Londonderry with an almost equally important branch off this to the port of Larne. It was natural that the MR would consider taking over the BNCR once the link via Heysham and its own fleet of new steamships was established, it is precisely what it did when it met other railways. It was in 1897 that the money for the Londonderry line of the DR became available so one is bound to wonder if its source was the fabulously rich MR on the look out for a suitable opportunity?

The MR took over the BNCR on very favourable terms to the BNCR shareholders in 1903, not as a wholly owned subsidiary, but as an integral part of its system, connected to it with MR ships from 1904 from Heysham. This made up about 12% (280 out of 2,170 route miles) of the MR's entire mileage. There were some local Irish concerns about the BNCR, a much loved company, being run from Derby so as a sop, the take over Act included the creation of the 'Northern Counties Committee'. This was a strange body with corporate existence but it did not own the railway, it was merely there to run and manage the former BNCR on behalf of the MR. But it did not own it; ownership rested directly with the MR, just as much as the MR owned any other part of its system. The Act required the NCC to have three local representatives, initially former BNCR directors, and three MR members, the power to appoint all six being resting with the MR. It met a few days before the MR's monthly board meeting, so that it could effectively communicate with the MR at Board level. It had a bank account for local use for revenue expenses and income, but paid all excess cash to the MR at Derby, from where any new capital required was provided.

Having built the Londonderry line, in 1902 the DR obtained the power to build the Ballyshannon branch by an act of 23rd June which also repealed the requirement for the separate accounting for the Londonderry and Ballyshannon lines and extinguished all government liability for guarantees on this and the earlier extensions. This meant that all the risk for the entire system now rested with the investors, making one would think it would be even more difficult to find investors on the open market. Despite the DR having spent all it had on the Londonderry line, private money mysteriously again became available, from where we do not know, to build the Ballyshannon line in 1903, which opened on 21st September 1905 barely a year after the MR took over the BNCR. Concurrently, the DR found itself able to pay for 22 superb new coaches, far better than the basic ones it had previously used, whilst a fleet of superb 4-6-4 and 2-6-4 tanks of the highest possible specification appeared effectively to equip it as a main line. This made it comparable with in terms of equipment and infrastructure, surprise surprise, the BNCR main line with which it connected at Londonderry. We cannot know if the MR had provided the required investment for all these developments, but perhaps not surprisingly, the MR then tried to take over the DR entirely. One is bound to wonder if the MR had been pumping money at the DR by way of loans, to get it ready for a take over in anticipation of the Heysham scheme and the BNCR take over? It is precisely what it did with, for example, the Midland & South Western Junction Railway, as impoverished a concern as one could find, until the MR lent it enough money to modernise, build a diversion and buy enough stock to make it in effect, a Midland route, to Southampton comparable with the Somerset and Dorset. The MSWJR though retained its independence, but that was no matter to the MR which through its investment effectively controlled the MSWJR for the rest of its corporate existence, indeed sorting out the loan from the MR (which approached £300,000 at one point) was the reason why the absorption of the MSWJR by the GWR was delayed until well after 1st January 1923 and why the LMS then had a significant shareholding in the GWR.

The GNR(I) objected to the DR takeover, as it would put the MR in direct competition with it not only for the Belfast to Londonderry traffic that had happened when the MR took over the BNCR, but also for the Strabane-Londonderry traffic, which line ran on the opposite bank of the river to that of the GNR(I) between the two locations. The solution was for the DR to be taken over jointly by the MR & GNR(I), as the County Donegal Railway Joint Committee. The GNR did not want the Londonderry line as it duplicated its own standard gauge route so this was taken over by the MR directly, owned, as was the BNCR, as part of the MR's own system. The NCC had no involvement in this ownership arrangement whatever. For convenience, the NCC did provide staff for the stations on the line from its 'pool' that also staffed the former BNCR. The NCC though did not operate let alone own the line, or any part of the CDRJC. The members of the CDRJC from the MR were Midland (3) and GNR(I) (3) nominees and as a general rule, the MR people were the same for the sake of convenience, who sat on the NCC representing the MR, but they did not sit on the CDRJC as NCC representatives, they were Midland men. The CDRJC operated the Londonderry line for a fee on behalf of the MR. This is the reason why railcars were rarely seen on the line, as the CDRJC was paid for running the trains so there was no need for economy on its part.

In 1902 a company was formed to build a line from Strabane to Letterkenny and the GNR(I) wished to contribute £72,000 but the balance of about £78,000 could not be found. However, the MR, clearly anticipating the DR take over, offered to join with the GNR(I) and provide more or less half the £150,000 capital for the S&LR, which they each did, along with a small minority of public and private holdings to make up the balance. But it remained an independent company with a separate board throughout its life, albeit operated by the CDRJC. Strategically, this meant that the MR & GNR(I) now had access to the traffic that arrived at Letterkenny from the far north of County Donegal and the Inishowen peninsular via the Londonderry & Lough Swilly Railway, with which the Strabane & Letterkenny connected at Letterkenny. As neither company had a convenient link to the LLSR at Londonderry this provided them each with the chance to syphon off traffic from the LLSR to their respective systems at Letterkenny via Strabane, and they did.

So there you have it. The CDRJC, jointly owned by the MR & GNR(I) owned the lines from Strabane to Stranorlar, Glenties, Donegal, Killybegs and Ballyshannon. The MR owned the Strabane to Londonderry line which was staffed by the NCC but operated by the CDRJC. The Strabane & Letterkenny line was owned by the Strabane & Letterkenny Railway Company, which was mostly

Londonderry and Lough Swilly Railway Class II 4-8-0 No. 12 approaching Letterkenny station on 18th June 1937.
PHOTO: © THE TRANSPORT TREASURY

owned in equal proportions by the GNR (I) and MR, but operated and staffed by the CDRJC.

This strange set up resulted in due course in the LMS replacing the MR. The NCC ceased to be in 1949 when the Ulster Transport Authority bought the former BNCR from the British Transport Commission but operated on its behalf by the Railway Executive, Northern Counties Committee, in effect a seventh region of British Railways. It was this weird set-up that resulted in Derby supplying the 2-6-4T 'Jeeps' to the NCC after nationalisation; the order had been placed before nationalisation and BR had no actual power to sell new locomotives to another operator, but as the materials had been ordered and the locomotives were being built, it was decided to complete the order, but not to provide such products in the future. Because the MR and then the LMS had owned the Strabane to Londonderry line, at nationalisation it became owned by the BTC directly, staffed by the NCC and operated by the CDRJC, which was half owned by the BTC. The sale by the BTC of the former BNCR by the British Transport Commission included at the BTC's insistence the Strabane-Londonderry line, despite the UTA not being keen to have it as part of a package deal. From then until closure the Londonderry line was owned and staffed by the UTA as successor to the NCC, but operated by the CDRJC, which remained half owned by the BTC as the MR's successor and the GNR(I). The UTA closed the Londonderry-Strabane line as fast as it possibly could.

On behalf of the British Transport Commission, BR (London Midland Region), on behalf of the British Transport Commission via the Railway Executive as successor to the MR/LMS jointly with the GNR(I) of the CDRJC, thus the Commission and its successors had a half share in a 3ft gauge railway that was mostly in the Irish Republic. The GNR(I) dropped out of the picture when it ceased to be, being replaced by CIE and UTA representatives, the GNR(I) having been split between the two organisations. Yet the CDRJC continued for many years after the railway closed, as did the S&LR, as there were pension complications in liquidating them entirely. As a consequence of the GNR(I) being taken over half by the UTA and half by the CIE, the CDJR was half owned by BR and a quarter each by the CIE and UTA. The Strabane & Letterkenny had the ownership proportions, plus a tiny minority interest. Eventually, the representational roles were taken over entirely by the CIE in return for cash payments from the UTA and BR, the same was done for the Strabane & Letterkenny and CIE paid off the minority interest. But legally the two companies (CDRJC and S&LR) remained in existence until the CDRJC and CIE pension schemes merged in 1981.

You also mention the Dundalk Newry & Greenore Railway, but simply say that this was operated from 1933 by the GNR(I). It was though a distinct company, owned entirely by the LNWR, then the LMS and then the BTC. Although closed in 1952, it was not dissolved as a company until 1957, neither CIE nor UTA wanted it, so the loss that it represented fell entirely on the British Transport Commission.

And then there were the LNWR interests in its own trackage and station at Dublin, served only by Irish railways, the huge investment that it made and retained by the LMS in the Dublin & South Eastern Railway, not to mention the strange ways that the LNWR came to own shares in the GNR(I), but life is probably too short for that.

If all this changes your allegiances to the GWR so you think that you've escaped this staggeringly complex story, think again. The GWR, via the still extant Fishguard & Rosslare Harbour and Railways company, partially owned railways in Wales and from Rosslare to Waterford, had huge investments in the Great Southern & Western Railway in Ireland, more or less owned the Cork City Railways and provided so much funding for the Waterford Limerick & Western Railway that it as good as controlled it in the same way as the MR did the MSWJR. Nor have we looked at the near take over by the LNWR of the Irish Midland Great Western Railway.

But we can save all this for another day.

YOURS, DAVID PEARSON, HAWORTH, WEST YORKSHIRE

Peter

Excellent first edition however one big error caption page 11 relating to page 10 photo this is 46237 'City of Bristol' not 'Salford', no cut down cab side sheets and of course together with No. 46236 she went to help out the Western Region during the 'Kings' bogie problems.

No matter a great start and I look forward to issue 2.

MARTIN HIGGINSON

An interesting Issue No. 1 but location of 'The Platform End' would have been informative.

MICHAEL THOMSON

Ed: I'm glad you found Issue 1 interesting and apologies for the oversight on my behalf for 'The Platform End'. The station is Blaenavon High Level, the photo being taken on 3rd January 1962.

SEND YOUR COMMENTS TO:

MidlandTimes1884@gmail.com

OR WRITE TO:

Midland Times, Transport Treasury Publishing Ltd., 16 Highworth Close, High Wycombe HP13 7PJ.

Hi Pete.

I wanted to congratulate you on your first issue of the Midland Times. This is a very worthy publication and sits well alongside the Western and Southern titles from Transport Treasury.

As my main area of knowledge is GWR and LSWR, I'm happy that there is now a publication where I can diversify that knowledge from a well written and researched publication.

I particularly liked the mix of articles covering a broad spectrum of interest. The typeface is different to other similar publications and works well, giving the Midland Times a somehow different, more appealing feel. I really think the typeface (and the writing style), sets the Midland Times apart from other publications. This really is a point of difference.

I wish the publication longevity and the success it so richly deserves. I'm very much looking forward to the next issue.

I'm also looking forward to the Eastern Times being available later in the year and I'm sure it will be equal to its Midland counterpart.

I have to say, that I'm a great fan of all of Transport Treasury's publications and tend to order anything new, as soon as it is published.

Keep up the great work.

Well done!

JOHN KALAITZIS, ADELAIDE, SOUTH AUSTRALIA

Dear Sirs

You have politely asked for constructive comment regarding Midland Times, so I decided to respond.

The content was nicely varied and interesting, particularly as I have an interest in the London electrification scheme.

Books are a very personal thing. With railways, I have always felt good quality maps and drawings help enormously, and there are a good few in this issue. The line drawings of Bath shed and Dalry shed are good and informative, but potentially could be even better, say if based on a background of an OS map, for example.

There's a good few photographs, could you add more? – especially with the line spacing used, if that was presented in a more 'traditional' spacing. The line spacing is the most distracting element for me – it looks like double-spaced typing for editors to correct – and so, inevitably, there is less content for the space.

I'm sure content will develop naturally with different contributors, but could there be included in each article who has written the piece, and source of information? You declare the book to be for 'students of the LMS…', suggesting a scholarly work, so references could be very useful.

I'm sure I've read elsewhere that such books are more likely to be read by people in relation to their modelling activities, and as such there surely could be continued scope for all manner of subjects covering the finer details of things, particularly with good quality photos and other illustrations. I'm looking forward to what is to come.

YOURS, ALAN COOPER